CUBA: A JOURNEY

Jacobo Timerman

CUBA

A Journey

Translated from the Spanish by Toby Talbot

ALFRED A. KNOPF NEW YORK 1990

·OI BOOK
PUBLISHED BY ALFRED A. KNOPF, INC.

Copyright © 1990 by Alfred A. Knopf, Inc.

Library of Congress Cataloging-in-Publication Data

Timerman, Jacobo.
[Cuba. English]
Cuba: a journey / Jacobo Timerman; translated by
Toby Talbot.— 1. ed.
p. cm.
Translation of: Cuba
ISBN 0-394-53910-9
1. Cuba—Politics and government—1959- 2. Cuba—
Description and travel—1981- 3. Human rights—
Cuba—History—20th century.   4. Timerman, Jacobo, 1923-
—Journeys—Cuba. I. Title.
F1788.T5313 1991   972.9106′4—dc20   90-53120
rev. CIP
Manufactured in the United States of America
First Edition

To Orville H. Schell

In Memoriam

CUBA: A JOURNEY

Prologue

If I had to sum up my long relationship with the Cuban Revolution, I'd say that I have always supported its right to defend itself from United States aggression—diplomatic, political, and economic—while I have at the same time criticized the violation of human rights and of freedom of expression that has characterized the Castro regime.

This, of course, is an oversimplification of a very complex history. The overthrow of Fulgencio Batista's dictatorship, the proud refusal to submit to Cuban and U.S. sugar oligarchies, drew my applause. It's impossible to forget that Cuba won its independence from Spain just after the turn of this century, only to be occupied militarily, politically, and economically by the United States until January 1, 1959, when the Revolution triumphed. Cuba was Spain's last colony in Latin America and the most profitable U.S. colony for a half century after that.

On the other hand, I personally experienced how disastrous it was to have the Cuban government supply arms and training to the left-wing terrorists who besieged my country, Argentina.

Nonetheless, the Castro government regarded me primarily as a prominent journalist, unswervingly and severely critical of the U.S. destabilization policy toward itself. More precisely, the Cubans perceived my attitude as one of affirmative ambivalence. And this tactical position accounted no doubt for the various official invitations I received in the course of twenty years to visit the island. But I consistently declined these invitations, for the same reason they were presumably offered: my simultaneous support and criticism. In any event, in over forty years as a journalist, only once did I accept a government invitation: from Great Britain, for I found it hard to turn down the request of the Crown's press attaché in Buenos Aires, a man whom I especially respected and esteemed.

To explain more specifically what the Cubans regarded as affirmative ambivalence, let me cite two examples. In two inter-American conferences held in Punta del Este, Uruguay, one in 1961 and the other in 1962, I defended Cuba's right to be considered a plenary member of the Organization of American States. As a commentator for Channel 9 television in Buenos Aires, I noted the positive attitude of Comandante Ernesto "Che" Guevara, Cuba's delegate to the '61 conference, regarding the nonideological spirit that ought to govern relations among members of the OAS. I even got to interview him briefly, though we'd had an agitated exchange of words at his huge press conference at the Hotel Playa in Punta del Este when I questioned him about the fate of religious schools under the revolutionary educational system. U.S. Secretary of the Treasury Douglas Dillon, on the advice of Latin American specialist Richard Goodwin, maintained an honorable position, ever searching for a peaceful solution. But at the 1962 conference, Latin American lackeys for the United States spared Secretary of State Dean Rusk the effort of barking in the face of the Cuban president, Osvaldo Dorticós.

My comments coincided with the efforts of the democratic Argentine and Brazilian governments, which opposed Cuba's expulsion from the OAS. Cuba finally was thrown out, and only Mexico maintained diplomatic relations with Havana. Over the years, I joined democratic Latin American leaders and numerous prominent United States liberals in demanding a reexamination of that action, which was contrary to the spirit and letter of the charter that gave birth to the organization.

Nor did my position go unobserved by anti-Castro terrorist groups. The Alpha 66 organization launched an aggressive campaign in San Diego, California, against my presence at the 1980 Inter-American Press Society Conference. I attended this meeting to report on the Argentine press situation under the military dictatorship from whose jails I'd been freed some months before. My friends advised me to leave San Diego for fear of an attack.

At no point did I regard my positions as contradicting the articles I published over the years demanding the freeing of political prisoners and the opening up of news. I particularly recall the great worldwide campaign to liberate the writer Heberto Padilla, which my newspaper, *La Opinión*, joined.

The other example of "affirmative ambivalence" occurred in Toronto in 1981, during a conference on human rights organized by Canadian intellectuals and Amnesty International. One of the committees compiled a list of writers throughout the world considered to be political prisoners. It was decided to draw up one general petition in behalf of all of them. This, in my opinion, would be a grand gesture but one without any concrete impact. I thought, on the contrary, that if there emerged from the conference an initiative that might gain the freedom of just one person on the list, that would constitute a genuine show of strength. Simone de Beauvoir, in *The Mandarins,* had already revealed her disillusionment with the automatic proliferation of manifestos. The Spanish Communist poet Rafael Alberti made a similar comment to me and my wife when, while we were visiting him in Rome, he was solicited by phone for yet another declaration on Chile. We all signed, but had doubts about how effective it was.

In Toronto, I proposed selecting one imprisoned writer and concentrating our efforts to obtain his freedom. I mentioned a man on the Amnesty list whom I'd never met or read but whose case was moving because of how young he was when imprisoned and how long he'd been confined: the Cuban Armando Valladares. The method of action I proposed couldn't have been simpler: we'd chain up the doors and windows of the Cuban embassy, demanding Valladares's freedom. The incident would attract substantial world coverage. On the other hand, if we petitioned in behalf of a long list of prisoners, we'd have to be resigned only to Canadian news coverage, with no one being freed. During my own imprisonments in military jails, I often had the fantasy that someone would chain the bars of an Argentine embassy for me.

It's curious how these kinds of meetings can, in the name of pluralist coexistence, fall under the control of the extreme left. The Uruguayan writer Eduardo Galeano led the attack against my proposal, and I suffered a bitter defeat. My only supporters were a Swedish delegate whose name I don't recall, and the writers Susan Sontag and Joseph Brodsky. All the imprisoned writers remained imprisoned.

Some time later, in London, Valladares's wife visited my hotel to thank me for the gesture. As I recall, she also brought a letter from the prisoner. I have never agreed with Valladares's ideas. After he was freed, he participated in United States diplomacy as a member of that country's delegation to the United Nations human rights conference in Geneva—just one more instance, in my view, of U.S. shortsightedness toward Cuba. Valladares, a man of the right, was reactionary, resentful, an instrument of a country that was not his own. But he had a claim to his freedom; his martyrdom in Castro's jails was indisputable; his dignity had been violated by the revolutionary regime. After he was released, to be sure, I saw no evidence that he was troubled by the violation of human rights in conservative dictatorships or in repressive, racist regimes. He is, as I said, a man of the right, and I am a man of the left, a socialist.

As a journalist, I maintained attitudes and positions that were not easy in a continent plagued by extremism, terrorism, the military, and the political ineptness of the powerful U.S. empire. I identified with Irving Howe's statement in the introduction to his book *Twenty-five Years of Dissent,* published in 1979: "To be a socialist in Europe means to belong to a movement commonly accepted as part of a democratic political life, a contender in the battle of interest and idea. To be a socialist in America means to exist precariously on the margin of our politics, as critic, gadfly, and reformer, struggling constantly for a bit of space. Lonely and beleaguered as it may be, this position of the American socialist has, nevertheless, an advantage: it forces one to the discomforts of self-critical reflection."

Though I'd been invited to Cuba in 1985 for the meeting convened by Fidel Castro to consider the foreign debt of underdeveloped countries, I had great difficulty in 1987 in obtaining a visa at the Cuban embassy in Buenos Aires. In 1985, my invitation was conveyed by Jorge Timossi, editor of the publishing house Letras Cubanas, who had worked on *La Opinión* before adopting Cuban citizenship. In 1987, I clashed with Jesús Cruz, political adviser and no doubt head of G-22, the Cuban secret service, in Buenos Aires. I can't describe it as a head-on collision. The embassy remained ambivalent; though it appeared the visa would be granted, it never materialized. Conversations resumed, but Cruz didn't seem to have a clear notion of what I might write about Cuba. He came to my house for lunch, we touched on all the usual topics, he was insistent on establishing the difference between *perestroika*— which I praised—and Cuba's Process of Rectification of Errors, which I did not know about in any detail. Mutual friends interceded in my behalf, or so I thought at the time, but the haze failed to dissipate.

Finally, I informed Cruz that I had to be in Madrid for a couple of days to attend to some last-minute details concerning the Spanish edition of my book *Chile,* and would find it convenient to take a return Iberia flight to Havana. He assured me that my visa would be waiting for me at the Cuban embassy in Madrid.

It wasn't. There were no instructions; no one had heard of me; the ambassador was unable to receive me.

The day I was to return to Buenos Aires, I had lunch with the Argentine ambassador in Spain, Hugo Gobbi, who took it upon himself to talk to the head of the Cuban diplomatic mission. Argentina's prestige was high on the continent at that time. President Raúl Alfonsín's government supported peace in Central America as well as Cuba's reentry into the Organization of American States and, above all, Argentine loans for Cuba. (In 1989, *Integración Latinoamericana* magazine, published by the Institute of the Inter-American Development Bank [INTAL], indicated that of the total debt then owed Argentina by other Latin American countries, 41 percent was Cuba's.)

There were several nervous, frantic conversations between Madrid and Havana, and several times I was told to be patient. As I was preparing to leave for Barajas Airport to board a plane to Buenos Aires, the Cuban ambassador phoned me at the Palace Hotel to inform me that I had just been granted a visa. My passport was subsequently stamped in Buenos Aires, and I departed for Havana on an Ilyushin plane of Cubana de Aviación airlines.

I, after all, had had an easier time of it than James Michener when he decided to visit Cuba. *Publishers Weekly* commented on Michener's trip: "It took him two years of bureaucratic struggle before he was allowed to go: the Cuban government doesn't look kindly on foreign writers visiting its shores."

Everything would have been simpler had I presented a definite agenda, including a complete list of people I wanted to interview and places I intended to visit. Moreover, the fact that I hadn't requested an interview with Fidel Castro drew attention. This was curiously expressed: To obtain an interview with El Comandante, I was told, one must request it well in advance. My reply surprised them: I wasn't planning to interview Castro. I must admit that I wasn't directly offered the interview at that juncture. The offer came later.

In fact, I'd already read countless interviews with El Comandante, and I didn't think that my questions would elicit any responses that diverged from the party line. Vanity of vanities, the idea of passing through Cuba without interviewing him appealed to me.

In January 1985, in the Spanish newspaper *El País,* Juan Luis Cebrián described his hours of conversation with Fidel Castro in Havana, and then on a plane flight to Managua and in the Nicaraguan capital. "Nothing happens if he personally doesn't conceive it, and this can range from organizing a conference of nonallied nations to a film festival," Cebrián wrote, referring to "that irrepressible proclivity of his to be the leading performer in his own show."

Castro, with an ambivalence that is more coyness than anything else, likes to complain about the role that is clearly, unanimously assigned him by journalists, writers, and politicians. He stated this emphatically in a conversation that went on, as usual, for many hours, over a three-day period, and was published in Havana in 1985, two years before my trip. The introduction to this volume, by the Cuban publisher, reveals many things about Cuban protocolar style that are reminiscent of other personality cults. It states: "Interviews granted by El Comandante in Chief, Fidel Castro Ruz, First Secretary of the Central Committee of the Communist Party of Cuba, President of the State Council, President of the Council of Ministers, to Dr. Jeffrey M. Elliot, adjunct professor of political science at North Carolina Central University, and Congressman Mervyn M. Dymally, Doctor of Philosophy, member of the Chamber of Foreign Affairs, and Founding President of the Caribbean-American Research Institute."

To a twenty-four-word question posed by Dymally regarding the desirable qualities of a leader and whether Castro had them, the latter responds with over three thousand words. I underlined the following paragraph: "I'm surprised that in the West, with presumably cultured societies, with thinking people, there's such a strong tendency to associate historical events with individuals and to magnify the role of individuals. I myself am aware of this: Castro's Cuba, Castro did this, Castro undid that. Almost everything in this country seems to stem from Castro, to be Castro's work, Castro's perversities. This type of generalizing mentality is, unfortunately, quite prevalent in the

West. In my opinion, it's an incorrect focus on political and historical events."

I accepted Fidel Castro's suggestion to exclude him, and to look for a Cuba without him. I attempted, in this manner, to get to know and to understand Cuba. Or perhaps I should say that I traveled to Cuba in order to get a sense of living in Cuba, to observe myself alongside Cubans, together with Cubans.

One day before leaving Havana, at the end of my stay, I met Comandante Emilio Aragonés, who had been the Cuban ambassador in Buenos Aires. He had not been informed of my presence on the island, even though I'd specifically asked to see this old acquaintance at the foreign press office of the Cuban chancellery. (Such top-level intrigues are commonplace in Cuba.) He suggested that I postpone my departure until he'd spoken to Fidel. Or that I return, for Fidel would lay out the red carpet for me at the airport. And he added: "I know what you've done for Cuba, and so does Fidel."

No, my trip had come to an end. But if I changed my mind, I assured him, I'd let him know.

One year later, toward the end of 1988, two Cuban colleagues visited me: Luis Báez, the political columnist of the official newspaper, and José Bodes Gómez, one of the directors of the official news agency, Prensa Latina. They invited me to participate, on January 1, 1989, in the celebration of the thirtieth anniversary of the Cuban Revolution, and possibly I could have an interview with Fidel. If the date was too close and I had other plans, a few months later they would be commemorating the anniversary of the establishment of Prensa Latina, and I'd be invited to Havana. "Heads rolled," said Bodes Gómez, when, after my departure, Fidel learned of my visit. Juan Luis Cebrián had understood the situation: "Castro molds his own image as leader with exquisite care. In the space of seconds he can be terrible, human, cruel, amusing, transcendent. He wants to know everything, to talk about everything, to give an opinion on everything." Tad Szulc, in his book *Fidel*, comments on El Comandante's inability to forgive Cebrián for using the adjective "cruel." That was the only thing that bothered him.

Yes, my trip had ended. I remained in Buenos Aires with my notes on Cuba, filled with memories, with feelings of hate, love, and nostalgia, and bearing inside me—forever, I am sure—the beautiful, fervid Caribbean island. I was in Cuba in the summer of 1987 and finished the writing of this book two years later.

Now the trip begins for you.

The Trip

The stout mulatto woman in her fifties was standing at the corner near the Hotel Presidente on the Avenida de los Presidentes. A hot August afternoon had just begun. About fifty yards away, a long line was waiting as usual for the bus. The woman was clutching a television set and sweltering from the heat. I was parking my car to go into the hotel, where I stayed most of the time I was in Havana, and the woman asked if I accepted fares. She was going to Old Havana, fifteen minutes away. She made it clear that she had no dollars, a necessary clarification in a city relentlessly fishing for tourists. Tourists aren't authorized to use the Cuban peso, whose bank value is one to one with the dollar, and seven to one when bought on the streets.

I told her I was only an Argentine tourist but that I had a couple of free hours and would be pleased to drive her. She climbed into the front seat without letting go of the television set, which she kept on her knees. She refused to put it in the trunk or on the back seat. She'd come from distant Santiago, 972 kilometers from Havana, to pick up the television that her children had sent her with a Venezuelan tourist. The visitor was staying at the Presidente; the woman's children had a pizzeria in Maracaibo, on the Venezuelan coast.

The woman invites me to the first-floor apartment in a run-down two-story building where she is staying with her sister's family; I am served coffee and a glass of water, and introduced to the family: the elderly brother-in-law, who is retired; the sister, an old woman seated in a rocking chair; the oldest nephew, a physician, who apologizes for being in his underwear and brings in his wife and infant; the youngest niece, an engineering student, seated on a sofa and reading old comic books published in Mexico in which Dick Tracy keeps brandishing his mighty fist. From a table I pick up a magazine similar to *Reader's Digest,* published in Moscow in Spanish, with themes and heroes long since buried by today's Soviet line.

The whole scene has an air of marginality, age, neglect. I'm received in the living room, whose high ceilings reveal in certain peeling sections its former colors; the walls are stained; broken panes on the wide colonial windows facing the street have been patched with cardboard; the meager furniture can barely stand up, so utterly pitiful and rickety are the pieces. Squalor, emptiness, monosyllables, prolonged silences.

I wait a discreet while for something to happen, to hear complaints, to be asked for help, to be questioned about the outside world represented by the television set, to hear the Revolution praised, to be asked to buy something in the shops for tourists and diplomats, which are inaccessible to most Cubans. There are only squalor, monosyllables, prolonged silences, failure, and a repressed joy in the discreet glances at the television set that has arrived from

Maracaibo. I say goodbye when it becomes quite evident that my presence is making them uncomfortable.

It occurs to me that *waiting* constitutes the inner dynamic of Cuba. Cubans are waiting for an outcome, a result, a finale. Those of us who go there are waiting too, hoping to discern clearly what it is the others are waiting for. When you arrive, having decided on the trip, you're convinced, or under the illusion, that objectivity and lack of bias will serve more than anything else to initiate a spontaneous dialogue with the Cuban people. You're waiting for some sensible statistic to eradicate the nightmare of hundreds of books, declarations, manifestos, all suspect of bad faith. You're waiting for some individuals in the streets of Havana, Cienfuegos, Trinidad, or Mariel to express themselves with a coherent awareness of what's happening in their lives and in the lives of their families; to shed some light on the confusion concerning the Cuban adventure that troubles both enemies and skeptics. You're waiting and hoping that in these streets, rather than in the offices of functionaries, the traps laid by fanatics and heedless individuals will spring open. You're waiting and hoping that the Cuban streets will be more lucid than the countless justifications brandished in the name of Latin American poverty to explain Cuba.

This at times seems possible. A friend called it "neither as happy as statistics say nor as unhappy as exiles in Miami say." I was reluctant to tell him that something much worse had happened to him: he was now a resigned man. My friend, too, had confined himself to waiting for the outcome.

I was in Cuba in 1987. In 1959, I had accompanied Fidel Castro from his press conference at the National Press Club in Washington to his enthusiastic meetings in New York, and to his appearance, shortly afterward, in Buenos

Aires. There he seemed slim, in a uniform beautiful in its youthfulness and modesty, as he stood near a vendor of barbecued beef in a place where workers had lunch on the shore of the sandy harbor of the Río de la Plata, etched against the hazy river that Jorge Luis Borges found so moving. He refused to acknowledge that Argentine workers regarded him with distrust and did not approach him because he had overthrown Juan Perón's great friend the dictator Fulgencio Batista. But still he was thrilled that the most beautiful women of the Argentine bourgeoisie kissed him because he'd overthrown that great friend of Perón, the Argentine dictator exiled from Buenos Aires a little over three years before.

I gazed intently at that young man, an individual without ideology who represented an eruption without a political program—one more of those violent eruptions that in Latin America are quickly, naïvely labeled as revolution. My generation, admirers of Augusto César Sandino and devoted to the Caribbean Legion started by Pepe Figueres, had more concrete enemies: Somoza in Nicaragua, Batista in Cuba, Duvalier in Haiti, Trujillo in the Dominican Republic. The Caribbean Legion had vowed to destroy them. Comandante Fidel had put an end to one of them. Buried in our nostalgia dating back to 1939, when we lost the Spanish Republic, we savored the word "Comandante." Never could those comandantes of ours be retrieved, those warriors with the flavor of the people. What had happened in Cuba—the eruption—meant that everything in the struggle toward a more just society, as we had conceived it, was possible: youthful idealists doing for the people exactly what should be done, with the unique strength that solidarity, generosity, and sacrifice provide.

Almost thirty years later, in Cuba, someone explained to me that the one with all the power is El Comandante, and young idealists await his order to follow him. This was not a political explanation, with statistical manipulations, tactical considerations, and historical strategies. It emerged from an unexpected, spontaneous dialogue with two girls about Bertolt Brecht, which occurred on the road between Havana and the Hemingway Marina. They were sweet the way young Cubans are, pupils at a drama school where Stanislavsky realism still holds sway.

Upon arrival in Havana, I'd rented what seemed to be the only air-conditioned car obtainable in Cuba. I waited a couple of days for a Mexican tourist and his daughter to return it to the state firm that handles all rental vehicles. When I went to get my accreditation from the foreign press office, which operated out of the Cuban chancellery, the aides tried to dissuade me from my plan of striking out alone in the streets and on the roads. But since I was an Argentine, speaking the language of the country, plus an amateur tango singer—tango music was incredibly popular in Cuba—what could happen to me?

I wouldn't know where to go, they said. But the fact is I had no set itinerary. I just wanted to talk with everyone.

Without the help of the press office of the Ministry of Foreign Affairs, they said, I'd be unable to get interviews with members of the government, of the academic world, or of principal organizations. I didn't want those interviews; I simply wanted to experience living in Cuban territory, free of commitments, immune to the virus of an agenda.

The CIA, just to create a scandal, they said, might make an attempt on my life. I couldn't see the CIA concerning themselves with me.

Two days later, with smiles but without congeniality, they gave me my accreditation. When my visit was over, I sent it to Robert Gottlieb, editor of *The New Yorker*, thinking that he might like to keep the first accreditation granted a writer for that magazine by the Cuban Revolution.

And so, one balmy morning I left Havana, heading west in my run-down Japanese car, which was vastly superior to the intolerable Russian Ladas that I'd withstood during a five-week trip through Nicaragua. I crossed the lovely avenues and gardens in the zone designated for embassies, eminent officials, and high officers of the armed forces, and kept going along Fifth Avenue, which leads to the road to La Boca and Mariel. I was hoping to get into one of those juicy dialogues with hitchhikers encountered on the road. The two girls had signaled with their thumbs, and there we were, traveling together.

Conversations with Cuban villagers are spontaneous when it comes to laughter, smiles, glances, pursed lips, hand gestures. But the words that come forth sound automatic. Words may embody contradictions. There's no danger of contradiction in a set speech. Words may reveal curiosity about experiences or anecdotes. No one sounds curious when delivering a speech. With words you can be questioned, or question another. In a set speech, a question is followed by an absolute truth, a resounding confirmation, unqualified approval.

In those two girls, I encountered that infernal mechanism I'd read about in the literature of Soviet dissidents. But on that balmy Cuban morning, their bubbly sensuality didn't coalesce with Stalin's ghost.

On the short trip, which I managed to extend to forty minutes, I perfected an antidote: Never again would I ask any confrontive questions. I'd begin a conversation with spontaneous confessions: stories about my life, my friends, my family, corners of faraway cities, poetry recitations, plans. Here, where the topic was theater, I found it helpful to talk about a weekend I'd spent at Arthur Miller's home in Connecticut, offer anecdotes about the Barraca

Theater, which García Lorca worked in, describe a play seen on a stage in Santiago, Chile, about Pablo Neruda's last days, speak of the sexual diversions of Clifford Odets. Which brought us to their current studies at the school of dramatic arts: Bertolt Brecht.

Journalism means allowing people to talk, but the girls barely spoke. I was carrying most of the conversation, watching their expressive faces, listening to their exclamations. I described the stage set of *Mother Courage* in Buenos Aires with the actress Alejandra Boero; I managed to hum one of Lotte Lenya's songs; long ago, I'd seen a film based on *The Threepenny Opera*.

The girls were studying the Marxist content of Brecht's work. His anti-Nazi struggle. His return to East Germany, where he had chosen to live, though he could have gone to Paris. But the girls' teachers, some of whom had been invited by European and American foundations, told them nothing about Brecht's endless irony, his corrosive, imaginative sense of humor. Nor had they mentioned Brecht's ongoing need to test how far Marxism could tolerate the impertinence of the desperate, the anguished romanticism of the Germans.

There were no questions, not the slightest tone of an interview. I simply claimed to find all this in Brecht, and much more. I spoke to them about Weimar Germany; the Spartacists; the assassination of Walther Rathenau; the German essence in Brecht. In this profession of journalism, one throws out names and places in order to note the significance registered on the other person. The girls were certain that that whole decadent world which I believed I saw passionately incorporated in Brecht's work, did not constitute part of the message. Brecht's inspiration came from the heart of the people, from his compassion for the people's suffering in war as well as in the exploitation imposed upon them by peacetime capitalism, and the content of his work was based on Marxist-Leninist ideas. El Comandante also loves Brecht.

"He loves Brecht?"

"For his devotion to the people."

The girls dismounted from the car, while I slowly continued on toward the seaport of Mariel. I stopped in the small square in front of a church. The priest, a Canadian, was in attendance only twice a week. That day he wasn't there. A girl had come to baptize her baby. She knocked in vain, looked through the windows of the house adjoining the church, walked back and forth, and then left. I sat down on a bench not far from an old man who was smoking in silence, watching over his grandson. Brecht would have treated those two beautiful, sweet-smelling girls humorously, amused at the flood of ideology spewing forth from two roses burnished by the Caribbean sun. He would have argued with them about El Comandante. Brecht's mordant pathos, his need to innovate, to modify, would have moved them more than El Comandante's hyperbolic declamations. If El Comandante aspired to destroy an old world in order to create a new one, I thought, this was not the time or place to understand Brecht in terms of his history, ideas, attitudes, and whims.

The girls had left me feeling empty. The old man barely spoke. He asked me for a cigarette and introduced me to his little grandson. He'd known a few Argentines in the past. He said nothing about the great exodus that had taken place in Mariel a few years before, when 114,000 Cubans departed from the port for Miami. He didn't evade questions. Simply, as often happens in Cuba, he didn't answer.

Brecht. Brecht. Perhaps in the confusing, frantic ideologic plot of the Latin American left, one has to revert more often to Brecht in order to survive with emotions more or less intact.

According to the Chinese, as is said in Cuba, certain dreams represent numbers, and these are numbers to place bets on. The horse is number one. That's why El Comandante is called The Horse. He has other titles too. I kept a page of the official newspaper *Granma*—it's redundant, of course, to say "official," since there's no other way to exist in Cuba, unless it be clandestinely—with a published letter from the Dirección Nacional de la Federación de Mujeres Cubanas (National Board of the Federation of Cuban Women) to: Compañero Fidel Castro Ruz, Commander in Chief, First Secretary of the Central Committee of the Party, President of the State Council, President of the Council of Ministers. The letter concludes with assurances that the membership is ready to "continue advancing under your guidance." Benito Mussolini had posters and stamps printed with his likeness, mounted on a horse and addressing the Italian people with the cry: "Follow me."

In the press, Castro's name is always, or almost always, accompanied by all his titles. Opponents, in dialogues held with me in difficult, mutually suspicious circumstances, preferred not to call him by name; stroking their chins, they'd refer to El Comandante. The most confirmed of Castro's adversaries are the ex-military—ex-companions in the Sierra Maestra, or participants in the battles waged in the cities against Batista. It was fiercer and bloodier in the cities than in the mountains. In the streets he's called Fidel, which sounds like camaraderie but more often proves to be an indifferent, noncommittal form of reference.

I learned this liturgy gradually, without asking questions, startling some by my occasionally uncontainable curiosity but handling it with extreme caution and considerable humility. I gained a more thorough understanding of this neurosis, which has become a natural reflex in Cuban society, in a lengthy conversation held at the home of an educated individual whose profession I can't name, whose living quarters I can't describe, whose religion I must not mention, and whose trying few days in a Havana prison cell I must not recall, as I must not the reasons for his arrest or the causes of his being freed. We were sitting in the living room of his half-demolished old mansion, in which there was a huge water tank to compensate for rationing, with a bucket alongside which had to be carried, half full, when you went to the toilet. (These details can't be used for identification purposes, since they apply to most dwellings.) Few things are as moving to portray as a house with a past and a soul, yet I'm obliged not to describe the outer friezes, the Spanish grillwork, the few remaining door-knockers, a bit of surviving molding on the doors. Or this curious professor. The radio blared away, and we spoke in whispers. He said that if I glanced discreetly out the window that he'd left open opposite me—he had his back to it—I'd see the window of a neighboring house where someone from the CDR, the Committees for the Defense of the Revolution, was surely watching us.

In the left-wing literature of Latin America, where I belong, such committees represented one of the purest expressions of the people in defense of the Revolution. Neighbors on every city street spontaneously kept watch from their own houses so that no one would threaten the victories achieved in 1959. But this man handed me a copy of the questionnaire that good neighbors are supposed to fill out and the CDR members are supposed to bring to the police, keeping a copy for themselves.

It's called *Boleta Recogida de Opiniones* (Opinion Collection Form), and a good revolutionary records what he hears from his neighbors and colleagues on the street, in the darkness of a theater, in the endless lines for milk, bread, or ice cream—even when he is unable to identify the speaker—or from his daughter's boyfriend or wife's cousin.

Under the item "Information on the Individual Expressing an Opinion," one is supposed to indicate the individual's age group (the questionnaire provides a space for each category: adolescent, up to 16 years of age; 17 to 29; 30 to 44; 45 to 59; 60 and over); the individual's sex; and the individual's occupation: professional or technician; executive; administrative employee; industrial or construction worker; service worker; unspecified worker; agricultural or fishing worker; private farmworker; worker in a cooperative; self-employed; soldier; student; housewife; retired; unemployed; unknown. Under the heading "Integration" there are only two categories: revolutionary; disaffected.

There are spaces, of course, for geographical location and date. But the most useful items of information for the police are requested in detailed form under the headings "Place Where Comment Was Made" and "Effect of Comment on Listeners." Place categories are: workplace; study center; residence; the street; place of business; recreation center; vehicle of transportation.

The item "Effect" is not very sophisticated: approval; disapproval; indifference. On the back of the form is a blank space for the text of the overheard opinion. At the bottom is a place for the signature of the—depending on one's view of this activity—revolutionary or informer.

Rather than organized informing, this is a collective state of mind in which the Cuban is, simply, a member or friend, a brother or son, of the Revolution and its Comandante—or else, an enemy of all. Even the most innocent, resigned Cuban, the most apolitical and defenseless, may heave a sudden sigh while standing on a long line under the sun, in front of a shoe store, and mention that his brother in Caracas, or his cousin in Miami, may soon be sending him some shoes. At the outset of the Soviet revolution, when Lenin was still accepting a measure of freedom of expression, and Ilya Ehrenburg was not as yet guided by Stalin's instruction, nor had he silently accepted the murder of his friend Isaak Babel, he wrote a novel about how Lazik Roitschvantz, weighed down by personal troubles, sighed at a public function while a Communist leader was making a speech which poor Lazik wasn't listening to. That sigh was the beginning of a prolonged imbroglio with the revolutionary police. This period of Soviet literature is of course unknown in Cuba. Reading about it could have spared the Cubans from repeating history. This time, however, the aphorism so dear to Marxists—when history repeats itself, it's first tragic and then comic—isn't fulfilled. What was tragic in the Soviet Union is today, seventy years later, tragic in Cuba.

El Comandante is knowledgeable about many things besides Bertolt Brecht, that eternal adolescent of a thousand antitotalitarian pranks. His knowledge in exercising absolute political power doesn't merely encompass the unlikely range extending from Brecht to the Cuban psyche. El Comandante has included psychoanalysis in his vast domain. It was El Comandante who, after speaking with Marie Langer, authorized the practice of psychoanalysis in Cuba. I wondered at the time what had prompted him to open the metal curtain with which Stalinist communism had excluded psychoanalysis. The revolutionary merits of Langer, perhaps, or El Comandante's self-image as Great Provider and Great Punisher. Marie Langer had undergone her analysis in Vienna in the early thirties with Richard Sterba, who had been analyzed by Sigmund Freud. As an adolescent, she joined the anti-Nazi movement. In 1932, she had observed in Berlin, where she did her studies, the emergence of Nazism. "On my return to

Vienna," she said in a kind of autobiography, "I began being militantly leftist. It seemed absurd to surrender without fighting." This was followed by service with the International Brigade in Spain, escape to Czechoslovakia, flight to Uruguay, and finally Argentina. The end of the war allowed her to throw herself totally into psychoanalysis, even though Peronism was upsetting: "I was very frightened when I heard a Perón speech for the first time; I thought of fascism." This occurred around 1946. In 1974, during Perón's third presidency, Marie Langer had to flee Argentina under death threat by the Fascist bands of the Triple A (American Anticommunist Alliance), which Peronism had organized. Taking refuge in Mexico, she visited Nicaragua periodically to participate in the training of psychologists, and she joined their crusade, begun at the 1969 International Congress of Psychoanalysis, in Rome, to have psychoanalysis admitted with full rights in a Communist society. I attended one of her classes at the Psychiatric Hospital in Managua. On another occasion, as she recounts, she had to confront questions that were posed by a full-fledged Sandinista psychiatrist: "So, Doctor, in what part of the brain is the seat of the unconscious?" Her friend the Argentine journalist Sylvina Walger recalled the moment, fifteen years after that Congress in Rome, when Fidel Castro told Marie Langer that she ought to "introduce this here." The old warrior had convinced El Comandante, or, more likely, El Comandante relished the possibility of exercising his power as Great Endower in the eyes of this exceptional, internationally respected human being. Marie Langer reported the event with party discipline but with scientific rigor. She wrote: "How can you teach psychoanalysis in a country like Cuba, which isn't going to accept an institute, or a four-year post-therapeutic psychoanalysis? These are unresolved questions. In any event, by gaining legal entry into the socialist world, we have, to some extent, un-expectedly, fifteen years later, changed the history of psychoanalysis."

In Cuba, one is informed daily that El Comandante's initiatives have produced historic changes in the cultiva-tion and harvesting of sugarcane, in housing construction, in military strategy in Africa, in language teaching, in street cleaning. When one displays curiosity about what prompts El Comandante to make speeches lasting for hours in certain neighborhoods or before television cam-eras, the reply is almost an offense to the intelligence of the person posing the question: El Comandante speaks in order to teach, he's a pedagogue, he resorts to the best form of collective education, for the citizens all pay atten-tion to him; it's the fastest way to educate. Those who believe that forcing people to listen to a single opinion on every subject has nothing to do with education are very wary—though perhaps decreasingly so—of the Opinion Collection Form employed by the Committee for the De-fense of the Revolution.

In my four weeks in Cuba, I was unable to rid myself of the depression produced in me by constant collisions with El Comandante's omniscience.

Any topic elicited a reference to some speech of his. The Soviet journalist Alexander Ignatov, from the Novosti agency, who in 1989 participated in an International Press Institute seminar on the relationship between informa-tion and ecology, described a situation that is currently the nightmare of those who want to write about Cuba, from inside or outside the country. Ignatov said: "Three years ago, in the Soviet Union, there were four rules gov-erning environmental problems: find your own informa-tion; statistics are forbidden; don't generalize from small problems; censorship."

The first step I took in Havana wasn't the obvious one

of getting my accreditation as a journalist. Back in 1960, as editor in chief of the newspaper *El Mundo,* and in 1971, as publisher of *La Opinión,* I had engaged the services of the official Cuban news agency, Prensa Latina. I thought that the editors of our international section should, without political bias, have access to all sources of news. But the material could seldom be used, since it was gross government propaganda, and perusing *Granma,* a newspaper I received sporadically, was simply a degradation of the act of reading.

These experiences prompted me in Havana to subscribe to the Spanish news agency Efe, which has a well-organized bureau there. Every day an envelope was delivered to my hotel with the service's complete report. This was, of course, also received by Cuban newspapers, radio stations, officials, diplomatic missions.

In the first half of August 1987, we were looking forward enthusiastically to the possibility of instituting peace in Central America. The presidents of five countries—Honduras, Nicaragua, Guatemala, El Salvador, and Costa Rica—had met in the Guatemalan city of Esquipulas at a summit, which succeeded, almost miraculously, in establishing an agenda that would allow its people to live in peace and democracy.

The day I arrived in Havana, President Daniel Ortega visited El Comandante to inform him of the details. There was a big news spread in *Granma* on the dialogue between the two chiefs of state, as well as comments on the role El Comandante played in Central American policy. Fidel Castro approved of the Esquipulas summit.

The envelope I received from the Efe agency quoted from a declaration by the Spanish prime minister:

MADRID, AUG. 14 (*Efe*). The head of the Spanish government, Felipe González, sent a message of congratulation and support today to the presidents of the five Central American countries, following the "positive results" of the Esquipulas summit meeting. Felipe González mentioned in his message that the agreement reached in Guatemala for the pacification of the region "opens promising perspectives for the strengthening of democracy and the economic and social development of the Central American nations." The Spanish premier "prayed that the political maturity that led to this agreement will continue to prevail in the future and, with everyone's participation, may successfully culminate the negotiations in progress in order to put into practice the agreed-upon commitments." Felipe González added in his message that they could always count on "the support and encouragement of the Spanish government for the attainment of this goal."

This news item was not published in Cuba. At the weekly press club meeting at the office of Interpress—a small press agency subsidized by third world governments—I was given a description of the very simple mechanism governing the publication of news presumed to affect Cuba's international policy: (1) you draw up a report to the Ministry of Foreign Affairs; (2) you wait for an answer.

"If the answer is long in coming?"

"You wait. The chancellery is flooded with work."

"If the answer doesn't come?"

"The item isn't published."

Felipe González's message, however, supported the Esquipulas agreement with the same enthusiasm as had El Comandante. No doubt about that.

"The chancellery has access to behind-the-scenes information that journalists lack."

The reason for dwelling on this silly anecdote is to illustrate why I'm furious, and why I express my fury without any attempt at the presumed balancing of what is good and what is bad that many of my leftist colleagues regard as objectivity, though it is at best simply childish ambivalence and, all too often, obsequiousness. It became clear to me at that point that Fidel Castro wouldn't share the stage the Esquipulas agreement lifted the curtain on—not even with an important friend. It was a question not of ideas or political strategies but of Castro's self-adjudicated role in the world and in Cuba.

During that time, the Argentine ambassador in Havana invited me for lunch at his residence, along with Ricardo Alarcón, vice-minister of foreign affairs. This knowledgeable man, who had spent many years with the Cuban delegation in New York, couldn't pursue an intelligent conversation on Esquipulas or the Latin American situation, because every argument had to conclude with an emphasis on the role Fidel Castro would play. I insisted, in vain, that supplying arms to Salvadoran guerrillas or maintaining an ideological hold on Daniel Ortega had no major influence on Latin American affairs. Señor Alarcón, knowing the role that Castro believed he occupied in world affairs, wasn't about to err in the role he was obliged to play in the presence of a journalist.

El Comandante's megalomania and this collective supporting hypocrisy is the dominant feature I encountered in Cuba: it defines society, the power structure, cultural life, work, family relations. No false or moderately credible statistic, no horrible past or promised paradise, no real or magnified threat, justifies this distortion of the elemental norms of human life.

Cuba has been confined in this alienating hypocrisy, and within such an impenetrable glass dome, survival isn't even a plausible battle or an imaginative activity. The alternatives are corruption and resignation.

While hypocrisy is first nature in Cuban society, ignorance is what constitutes its nervous system. The statistics regarding the victory over illiteracy are infuriating and harrowing. If it is true that every Cuban knows how to read and write, it is likewise true that every Cuban has nothing to read and must be very cautious about what he writes. In the bookstore on Twenty-third and L streets, opposite the Habana Libre Hotel, the shelves are overflowing with the Spanish editions of books by Russian writers. The same occurs in the most important bookstore, a few yards away from the Floridita restaurant, the place where Ernest Hemingway drank daiquiris in Old Havana. I spent a few hours watching Cubans acquire works that Soviet historians and writers nowadays criticize as falsifications of Soviet reality. The spectacle is pathetic. One month before the celebration in Moscow of the seventieth anniversary of the October Revolution, Havana bookstores were offering Cubans an anthology of the greetings received by the Kremlin on its sixtieth anniversary. The scene struck me as a symbol of the sclerosis of a regime unable to accept modifications of any sort. It is anchored down.

Books are very cheap, more so perhaps than in any country in the world; but they are a denigrating hoax. And this, too, is part of the all-pervasive hypocrisy. The newspaper *Novedades de Moscú* (Moscow News), which is published in Spanish in the Soviet Union and promotes *glasnost*, didn't enter Cuba in sufficient quantity to supply all those lining up at the newsstands for a copy. (I saw photocopies circulating among the few activists devoted to human rights.) It became for Cubans a kind of *samizdat*, but even those who could enjoy it didn't dare to include its topics spontaneously in conversation.

On his seventieth birthday, in 1983, Carlos Rafael Rodríguez, vice-president of Cuba and the Communist who lent his party's support to Castro's guerrillas in the Sierra Maestra—at a point when his comrades were defining Castro as a bourgeois adventurer—granted an extensive interview to the Cuban journalist Susana Tesoro. *Bohemia* magazine published it in its May 1983 issue:

Tesoro: "Which are your favorite authors and texts? Which are your top books?"

Rodríguez: "Maybe I'd choose a selection of Martí, for its evocative power. Of course, among writers my preferences would probably be Faulkner over Hemingway, though I admire both; I'd choose Shakespeare over Tennessee Williams or García Lorca; Günter Grass and García Márquez, though detesting the former as a political being and loving the latter as a best friend."

This response presents an interesting pluralistic literary panorama, but one that is accessible only to those authorized to visit outside Cuba. I went through the bookstores in Havana and was unable to find a single copy of Faulkner, Williams, or Grass. Furthermore, under the island's impenetrable glass dome there are no Cubans of average education with the slightest notion of who these authors are. The name *A Streetcar Named Desire* evokes Marlon Brando among some with a good memory.

Five years after the Rodríguez interview, in 1988, the leftist Argentine newspaper *Página 12* (Page 12) reproduced an item from the Cuban newspaper *Juventud Rebelde* (Rebel Youth): "At the end of the year, perhaps, or at the beginning of the next, there may appear a series of highly prestigious titles in contemporary literature and other milestones in world literature of the last decades. . . . Among the titles in question are *The Tin Drum*, by Günter Grass, and *The Name of the Rose*, by Umberto Eco."

There is much literacy in Cuba and too much printed paper. At the time of the *Juventud Rebelde* announcement, the Cuban magazine *Somos Jóvenes* (We Are Young) published a survey on reading habits, and one student's answer was: "Yes, the bookstores are full, but you don't always find something to buy." The Cuban writers Leonardo Padura, Miguel Mejides, and Norberto Codina—according to an Agence France Presse cable, also published in *Página 12*—told the Havana newspaper *Trabajadores* (Workers) that publishing houses "prefer to stick to their annual plan of printing one hundred thousand copies of three titles instead of publishing one hundred titles in editions of three thousand copies." The three writers felt that "we are forty years behind in foreign literature."

Gabriel García Márquez, of course, is uncensored, except when he enthusiastically refers, as he often does, to *perestroika*. His famous dialogue with Mikhail Gorbachev at the Moscow Film Festival in 1987, transmitted by Soviet news agencies, was not published in the Cuban press. The Colombian writer is the man who can perhaps influence Fidel Castro most. He is El Comandante's most important instrument of public relations on the international front. His personal interventions with Castro have achieved certain freedoms, though his repeated appeals for an improvement of quality in the Cuban press have failed totally. Anecdotes frequently circulate in Latin America about García Márquez's whispered criticism, in endless private conversations with Fidel Castro, of the Cuban state of affairs. But this confidential whispering, according to versions both men relay to intimates, seems more like complicity than an act of conscience when compared with the magnitude of García Márquez's public eulogies with their byzantine hyperbole.

At the beginning of his novel *Darkness at Noon*, completed in 1940, Arthur Koestler quotes a remark by Louis

Antoine de Saint-Just, the relentless young French revolutionary of 1789: "He who rules is guilty." In the story of the trial, sentencing, and execution of Nicholas Rubashov, Koestler describes the Moscow trials of the thirties, the facts of which were confirmed by contemporary revelations in the Soviet press about the execution of the 1917 revolutionaries Bukharin, Zinoviev, and others. Perhaps it's inevitable for the one who rules to turn out guilty, but Koestler proves that being a writer doesn't inevitably include being an accomplice.

Reading the foreword written by Gabriel García Márquez for the book containing Gianni Minà's interview with Fidel Castro for Italian television reminded me of Koestler's books and the attitudes of some of his contemporaries. Pablo Picasso drew a portrait of Joseph Stalin that genially captured the image of a revolutionary leader, although the French Communist Party of that time would have preferred something more classical, displaying Stalin's presumed generous, brave, just personality, and also his wisdom as depicted in the poems of the Chilean Pablo Neruda, the Argentine Raúl González Tuñón, the Peruvian Alberto Hidalgo, the Turk Nâzim Hikmet.

Such obsequiousness may perhaps be excused to some degree in light of the great battle being waged at that time against fascism. But the observations in *Darkness at Noon* and the publications of Soviet historians and journalists under the sway of *glasnost* show clearly that it was Stalin, Stalinism, his accomplices and followers, that made possible the initial triumphs of fascism.

What's fascinating about García Márquez's prologue to that sixteen-hour interview is not its political content but its similarity to the driving mechanism that prompted those previous intellectuals to claim that one human being can actually possess the combined virtues ascribed to Stalin—the same virtues presently bestowed by the Colombian upon Fidel Castro.

In the light of *glasnost*—Minà's book containing the Castro dialogue was published in 1988—this prologue is rash, indecent, infantile. García Márquez praises Fidel Castro for needing only six hours of sleep after an intense day of work. The same six hours were often presented as proof of Joseph Stalin's vitality, extolled in writings that described his Kremlin window, lit until the wee hours. García Márquez praises Fidel Castro's wisdom in stating that "learning to rest is as important as learning to work," a remark of the same force and originality as the recommendation appearing in the free almanacs in apothecary shops of old: "Idleness is the mother of all vices."

If the cumulative tasks in Fidel Castro's workday, as described by García Márquez, are methodically enumerated, the figure emerging is a Rambo, someone who triumphs owing to his supernatural intelligence, someone without need to resort to the weapons Hollywood places in the hands of that quintessential American Fascist. García Márquez says of Fidel Castro that "his rarest virtue is the ability to foresee the evolution of an event to its farthest-reaching consequences"; "he has breakfast with no less than two hundred pages of news from the entire world." (Just try to read two hundred pages in the time it takes to have breakfast.) Moreover, "he has to read fifty documents" daily. "No one can explain how he has the time, or what method he employs to read so much and so fast"; "a physician friend of his, out of courtesy, sent him his newly published orthopedic treatise, without of course expecting him to read it, but one week later he received a letter from Castro with a long list of observations"; "there is a vast bureaucratic incompe-

tence affecting almost every realm of daily life, especially domestic happiness, which has forced Fidel Castro
himself, almost thirty years after victory, to involve himself personally in such extraordinary matters as how
bread is made and beer distributed"; "he has created a
foreign policy of world-power dimensions." Thus Fidel
Castro has a secret method, unknown to mankind, for
reading quickly; and he knows a lot about orthopedics;
yet thirty years after the Revolution he hasn't managed
to organize a system for distributing bread and beer. But
the mere fact that El Comandante is personally involved
in the problem represents one more virtue added to the
long list of his other virtues; he foresees the future;
knows how to work and rest; his sleep is of the same
duration as Stalin's, and, as happened with Stalin, he is
transformed into an all-knowing truth-seer and ever-tri-
umphant conquistador by one of the greatest writers of
his time.

Who is the victim? Not Fidel Castro. Nor Gabriel García
Márquez. In Pablo Neruda's complete works, poems on
Stalinist glory don't appear. Stalin's portrait is an insig-
nificant detail in Pablo Picasso's work, and few recall it. In
García Márquez's complete works, at some future date,
and not under Fidel Castro's surveillance, to be sure,
the perishable prologue to Gianni Minà's book will not
appear.

But there are victims, millions of victims: the young
people who devour everything that García Márquez
writes, without recourse to the slightest defense that experience and memories provide, or access to more open
cultural spheres. They will readily accept, because the
author of *One Hundred Years of Solitude* says so, that
there dwells in Havana a magical being who will lead
them to victory, for he is omnipotent and all-knowing.
And they will allow themselves to die in some guerrilla

or terrorist enterprise without having the opportunity to ask García Márquez what he thinks of Arthur Koestler. It is unfair.

Anyhow, it's two in the afternoon of just another day, and I'm in Cumanayagua. I'd left Havana thinking I was headed southeast toward Trinidad, the old Spanish port on the southern coast, but I took the wrong road. It was near Santa Cruz del Norte, I believe, that someone signaled to me on the road and asked to be taken to a certain intersection. He, too, was heading south, and we proceeded together on the road I had missed. He got out near Amarillas. Farther along the road, a girl got in and indicated on my map that if I was going to Trinidad, she'd leave me at Cienfuegos, where a secondary road would take her to Cumanayagua. She was coming from Havana and wore a yellow T-shirt with the inscription "Catch a Guy." That night, after covering something like four hundred kilometers, stopping at various places—I had to wait at a bar for one of the customers to empty a glass before I could get a beer—I made a notation: "Vegetation and landscape, Caribbean; music and sensuality, African; language, deriving from Spain; but the daily lifestyle is as American as the glass dome allows." Since the bar was not for tourists, I was able to pay in Cuban pesos, which I'd bought out of curiosity from those boys who hang around hotels, devoted to the black market in foreign currency. Of course, there is never a shortage of glasses in places where only dollars can be spent.

There exists in Cuba a proliferation of unverifiable statistics, as well as predictions. The government estimated that nearly 200,000 tourists would arrive in 1988 and that by 1991 there would be 600,000. But on July 26, 1988, the anniversary of the attack on Moncada barracks, Cubans, while listening once again to Fidel Castro declare that Cuba continues to be a true and perhaps the only genuinely authentic socialist country, were also informed that they would not be permitted to use the hotels and facilities reserved for foreign tourists. Tourism presumably will represent Cuba's second source of income after sugar, and, said El Comandante in his inevitable speech, "only a petit bourgeois dandy is unable to understand why Cubans can't use those rooms." The bars set aside for Cubans will remain without drinking glasses.

I discussed the subject of tourism with Vice-President Rodríguez. I'd applied for an interview just after my arrival in Cuba, but the chancellery never answered me. By chance, at the end of my stay, a Cuban I'd met in Buenos Aires managed to obtain an appointment for me. Rodríguez was the only official Cuban personality I made an attempt to meet. I knew about his culture, good humor, sophistication, and pluralism. He was one Cuban who could take some of the cataclysmic slogans of the bureaucracy as a joke. We spoke about the importance of tourism for Cuba, and I suggested that significant earnings in foreign currency could not be expected from the current subsidized tourism. A tourist of means wants places to spend money, newspapers and magazines to read, nightlife, available young women and men. All tourism brings a measure of corruption, or at least great liberality in customs, as witness Spain, Greece, Israel. Indeed, he said, this was foreseen, and Cuba was prepared for certain things, such as allowing the entry of *Time* and *Newsweek*, some United States, Canadian, and European newspapers, a certain amount of nightlife. But it would not tolerate what goes on in Varna, the bathing resort on the Black Sea, where Bulgarian youths go to bed with mature German women just to get a pair of jeans. I suggested to Don Carlos Rafael that before coming to a decision, he should consult Cuban young people.

The girl driving with me didn't get out when we passed Cienfuegos, because I insisted on driving her to Cumanayagua, some twenty kilometers to the east.

On my worktable, I have pictures I took of the girl and of her family home. As I'm writing, I must be careful not to harm her by this account, though nothing particular was said, nothing that had the slightest political connotation. That, perhaps, was what was so significant about it.

A small wooden house in which grandparents and, perhaps, great-grandparents had lived long ago. Inside, three rooms, meticulously painted, a dilapidated outhouse in back to cover the hole in the ground that serves as toilet. The girl pumps water into a bucket for me to bring to the outhouse. She pumps a little more into a washbasin, gives me some soap, and I wash my hands. In consolation, she mentions that it's worse in the city of Cienfuegos, where apartment buildings with running water are supplied only six hours a day, and pans of water must be stored in the rooms. Here there is always water running in the underground streams below the village of Cumanayagua. I am given some coffee and a glass of water.

The father died fighting in Angola, and the family was awarded a medal by the Army. The burial was in Angola, since the government didn't repatriate the bodies. Various explanations were offered me in Havana concerning this failure to repatriate the dead: the cost, the climate of despair that would be created in local cemeteries, the recurrence of that mood on the anniversaries of the death. Possibly there were other reasons, none of them satisfactory. There's nothing exceptional about this: I saw a cemetery of British soldiers on Mount Scopus in Jerusalem, one of American soldiers in Italy, another of Spanish resisters

Macbeth, which are devoted exclusively to the tango. Merry Cubans enjoy this sad music, those anguished, melancholy verses that speak only of failures and betrayals and that sprang from Buenos Aires brothels almost a century ago.

I spend a couple of hours with them, then continue on to Trinidad. I stay at a hotel overlooking the sea a few kilometers from the city.

Many times afterward I thought about that girl and looked at the five snapshots taken on that visit. A friend of mine, warning me that not everything in Cuba is a message, had remarked derisively that some things are simply a massage. What I found most poignant, perhaps, was that conclusions can't be drawn from a few brief hours of sheer, honest humanity. One just can't jump to conclusions. Nonetheless, I feel that there was something else.

No one in the little wooden house in Cumanayagua expressed any desires or dreams. Is such passivity normal? During a long encounter, won't certain anxieties surface, the dream of attaining something remote, a longing to be elsewhere? Were we not weighed down by a tombstone, a conclusive event, a situation in which everything was predetermined? Cuba seems like a consummated situation, and I feel that in some important sense I failed this girl. It would have been hard, but even in Cuba, in that remote, wretched place amid green tropical hills, I should have found some way of shaking off the passivity, of enriching the monotony, of casting a bottle into the sea, of issuing a warning, of establishing some connection for them with the outside world.

They asked for nothing, I offered nothing, no link was established despite the fact that the three of us, that afternoon in Cumanayagua, loved one another. To this day, when trying to envision the link that should have sponin France. The difference is that Cubans can't visit the graveyards in Angola.

No one asks me any questions, but they are amused by my stories about Argentina, about Evita Perón. I suggest having dinner together, but the girl, laughing, shows me that the icebox is empty. Her gaiety is contagious, like that of all Cubans. Through the windows, I see some neighbors walking by to look at the unexpected Japanese car stationed next to the humble dwelling. They probably assume, says the girl, that it's a diplomat's vehicle. It occurs to me that we could go and buy some food, some provisions, a bottle of rum, a lobster. But there are no tourist stores in Cumanayagua. Those set aside for Cubans are closed at this hour. Besides, there's rationing. The girl goes outside to a small plot of land in back, where the outhouse is, and pulls two fruits from a tree. We eat guayabas.

There's also a television set, two dolls, and a double row of assorted empty bottles adorning some shelves. A plant hangs from the ceiling. The mother hasn't remarried, the two sisters are divorced, and the girl is engaged. She's studying in a school in Havana, where she lives; she is graceful, charming, and animated. I suggest that she dance a bit, and sing. I tell her that I'm falling in love with her even though I'm almost half a century older than she is. The mother laughs. The girl says that the mother is the most beautiful of them all and that we'd make a fine couple. I show them a picture of my wife and grandchildren, and we laugh some more.

The girl wants me to sing for her mother the tangos we sang on the trip. I feel a bit ridiculous. A Ukrainian Jew in his sixties, almost bald, gray-haired, fat, whom Cubans ask to sing tangos but not if he knew Che Guevara. Being taken for a Río de la Plata macho can be difficult. The family often listens to the radio broadcasts of María Luisa taneously, firmly been forged, I'm unable to come up with the formula to have made it possible. It's strange and painful, that distant landscape of such splendid people subject to a definitive, conclusive event, lacking the logical reflex of grasping at someone who doesn't belong to the established, learned, incorporated, biologically transformed norms. It is unjust.

I got my hotel room in Trinidad thanks to my journalist accreditation. It is summertime, and the place is filled with Cubans. (A hotel for foreigners will soon be installed nearby, in Ancón.) According to the price list, a guest is entitled to a discount on days when there's no water or no light, or in rooms with air-conditioning that isn't working. The swimming pool has no running water; entering it is like going into a Turkish bath, but off to one side, against a wall, are showers for cooling off.

I tour the old section of the city of Trinidad, maintained as a museum just as the Spaniards left it in its period of greatest opulence. Fleets bearing the spoils of America to Spain gathered in that port. As I'm filling the car's tank with gasoline obtained by using special vouchers bought with dollars, a mestizo man of around fifty approaches to ask if, by any chance, I'll be passing through Cienfuegos. Yes, since I'm going to Havana. He has his ticket for the bus that picks up passengers right on this street, but judging by his number, it would surely be seven hours before he reached Cienfuegos, about eighty kilometers from Trinidad. He is a worker in a petroleum refinery and lives where he works: a "live-in worker," with no residence, who boards in special refinery dormitories. On weekends he relies on an improvised bed in the family home where his mother, sister, and two nephews live. He sleeps in his nephew's room. He's divorced through his own fault; his wife wouldn't forgive all his "partying." He's proud that his three children have been able to study and are professionals. No, he doesn't live with them, because at this moment they, too, are "live-in workers."

I was in another house as well, some distance from Cumanayagua: that of the Argentine Fernando Birri. We were friends in our distant youth. Now he dresses like an orthodox monk, wears a bizarre hat of exclusive design, has a long beard, is rather dirty, and heads the International School of Film and TV in San Antonio de los Baños, about forty kilometers from Havana. The students live at the school. Birri's house, in Reparto Flores, a residential area of Havana, has two floors, a private beach, a garden and terrace overlooking the sea; he has been allotted an official car with a chauffeur, and two servants. His is one of the "protocol houses" reserved for friends or special guests of the regime. On the wall is a painting by the Cuban Manuel Mendive, a gift from the minister of culture. My attention is caught by the strange depiction of human and animal forms, particularly the recurrence of open mouths, creating as it were a universe of oral appetites and expressions: a kind of orality catapulted toward symbolic extravagance. A few days later, I visit Mendive's exhibition of paintings and sculpture at the National Museum of Havana and go to his studio, an hour from the city, in Reparto Dulce Nombre in the village of Cotorro. I didn't find him. I waited an hour. It was impossible for me to arrange an appointment, for he had no telephone.

Fernando and I recalled old friends, especially the writer Beatriz Guido and the filmmaker Torre Nilsson. I thought I'd find him predisposed to elaborate for a journalist on the great adventure of directing a school whose goal is to create a third-world cinema. But he's somewhat uncertain of how to pigeonhole me. In order to provide a clearer sense of the new institution, he hands me a copy of the "Founding Declaration of the International School of Film and TV of San Antonio de los Baños, Cuba, also known as the School for the Third World." And to emphasize the importance of its task, he passes on a comment of El Comandante's. Fidel Castro had declared that thanks to an extensive report on the school in the pages of *Il Manifesto,* a prestigious publication of the independent Italian left, Cuba again has a prominent position in that daily. Fernando had learned quickly to value a favorable opinion from Fidel Castro. I couldn't resist reminding him that many years back, in our youth, it was important for an Argentine filmmaker to have La Señora be enthusiastic about a film. La Señora was Eva Perón. We agreed that Evita had not given birth to the socialist revolution, though I don't think we had the same thing in mind.

I find Fernando thinner, emaciated, ill, but enthused because García Márquez has entrusted him with the filming of one of his works. Special meals are prepared for Fernando, and his medications come from abroad via friends who travel. Getting a conversation going is futile. His speech is a nonstop rant, and I'm unsuccessful in grounding it on any terrain where mutually acceptable codes might apply. His incoherent mixture of magic, sociology, third-worldism, plus brief whispered interpolations of who's who in Cuba and the intrigues being woven to depose him as head of the school, reminds me suddenly of Ezra Pound, without the poetry or genius but with a torrential replication of Pound's personal dictionary, all his words and inflections.

In Havana, I devoted no time to investigating how this ailing quack managed with his chaotic terminology to convince Fidel Castro, Gabriel García Márquez, and Hollywood's guilty consciences, Robert Redford in particular, to finance and support this attack of madness. But someone in the industry who protects the school should be questioned on the film work and the filming difficulties encountered by the most talented of Cuban directors, Tomás Gutiérrez Alea. One might think that after twenty-two years, as the veils concealing rigid European Communist society are being lifted, the answers to such questions wouldn't be hard to find. Not everyone feels obliged to offer Fidel Castro such words as are contained in the school's Founding Declaration, words that reaffirm for El Comandante that he occupies a unique, inaccessible position in the evolution of the universe. I've extracted a few paragraphs from the declaration.

> Early in the warm spring of '86, surrounded by the turquoise-blue Caribbean, beneath the rising moon, the Foundation of New Latin American Cinema, shipwrecks from Utopia, salvaged from a world of imperial injustice and atomic madness, resolves to create the International School of Film and TV in San Antonio de los Baños, to be known also as the Third World School (Latin America and the Caribbean, Africa and Asia).
>
> This school, the result of needs, experiences, and self-critical reflections achieved over 30 years of New Latin American Cinema, was, prior to its existence, merely an idea traveling from desk to desk, represented only by its graphics, three superimposed shapes: a circle, a blue square, and a yellow triangle, which now have become the logo of this atypical school. Atypical as implied by its synthesized logo and, despite its name, a school that is not academic but anti-academic; a center to generate creative energy for audiovisual images. (A factory of the eye and ear, a laboratory of the eye and ear, an amusement park of the eye and ear). . . .

... it is a true Cinema and TV city, built by the 25th Anniversary of Girón Construction Brigade, 300 volunteer Cuban comrades, working day and night, in San Antonio de los Baños, thirty minutes outside Havana, amid a row of palms, as if to reinscribe those buildings with Leonardo's old motto: *Ostinato rigore,* ... though our own Nobel Gabo, less academically and more vigorously, might prefer the motto: *Let us dance and make merry with the National Symphony.*

The declaration goes on to indicate that the "Nobel Gabo" is Gabriel García Márquez, winner of the Nobel Prize for Literature and president of the Foundation of Latin American Cinema.

A few more paragraphs:

Through evil colonial policies that divided and separated us from self-rule, and further separated by ocean-years, mountain-years, desert-years, forest-years, the time and place have now come, imbued by the Absent Interlocutor: the Latin American and Caribbean brother, the African and Asiatic brother, with whom we share the burden of anonymity, to multiply the voltaic, electronic light of our convictions. . . .

In short, to define ourselves, perhaps, to gain self-awareness in our free quest for utility, truth, and beauty ("Within the revolution of beauty everything, outside the revolution of beauty nothing"), inasmuch as the nullification of political-poetic pseudocontradictions may find in us all, present and future, no mightier expression than militants of the image. Like magma beneath the volcanic oxides of Momotombo, there are two subjective impulses, two historic aspirations underlying the rational masonry of this project. They are, fundamentally, diastole—everyone's right to life: the stomach of life, the dignity of the stomach. And systole—the right to the image: the dignity of the image, everyone's right to satisfy a hunger for the image. . . .

Illumined by flashing swirls of Caribbean foam and by the pulsation of spy satellites, false stars of audio-visual penetration which will not impede the oncoming dawn of our struggles for liberation, in that orgasm of birth of the collective imagination, a long life to the Utopia of the Eye and Ear of the International School of Film and TV in San Antonio de los Baños, Island of Cuba, the reunion of Three Worlds.

Fernando Birri is a typical Castroist. As is the entire bureaucracy of the country. After the recent Polish experience, it isn't hard to predict that in a free election the candidate Fidel Castro would receive less than 10 percent of the votes. And Cuba's economic situation is a greater catastrophe than was Poland's at its worst moments. Despite this, the bureaucracy handles the Castro line very well, though never as effectively as Castroists going back and forth from abroad. It's logical. Foreign Castroists have all the motivations and none of the hardships. They cling to Cuba as a way of not accepting that the socialism they grew up with has crumbled with a resounding crash and that new forms are emerging. Castroism still presents themes and symbols which are getting loudly and publicly buried in Communist countries: the imminence of a nuclear war between the United States and the Soviet Union, or simply the U.S. threat to a way of life; the injustices of the market economy; the degradation of the consumer society; the capacity and sacrifice of populist heroes; the word "revolution" and its concomitant idols.

Castroists manifest some progress when they admit the

danger of a total breakdown of Cuba's economy, the deterioration of the quality of life for those on the island, but these they absorb as the difficult moments any revolution and every country must undergo. They exhibit a serious, almost pathological incapacity in the way they gloss over difficulties, separating them from the country's ruling structure: refusing to try to examine the structure of that society, apart from its acute shortages or hardships.

Saul Landau, the American filmmaker and writer, in an occasionally objective piece in the July–August 1989 issue of *Mother Jones,* describes a visit to Cuba in December 1988, with details from a filmed interview with El Comandante. Landau writes: "As Fidel spoke, I allowed myself to listen closely and feel that peculiar sensation I experience in his presence, as if I am meeting with a force of nature, a man so filled with the energy of historical mission that he is almost of a different species. Power radiates from him, emitting acute awareness of his needs—and a realization of how closely these needs have related to the destiny of his nation."

In fact, Landau, like many foreign Castroists, intimates that Castro has accomplished his glorious mission: "The Cuban people have achieved sufficient maturity to govern themselves, I thought, even without the presence of their leader, their guide, their Solomon and Hercules."

Herein lies the center of the drama being played by foreign Castroists, who don't have to belong to the regime's bureaucracy in order to survive, but whose calling is authentic. The crucial question is not Castro, who, despite what Landau says, belongs to the same species as we do, with the same biological limits. The question is how to analyze that glorious mission which Castro, from the viewpoint of these Castroists, so totally fulfills. It is a collapsing formulation if you reiterate a very simple lesson from history: A nation's right to self-rule is not a matter of whether or not it has reached the maturity to do so; it is simply an inviolable right.

It would take more than a Freudian or Lacanian psychoanalyst to explain why non-Cuban Castroists accept the demythification of the Communist leaders of Eastern Europe and China but remain mesmerized by El Comandante. "Their teacher, their guide," are ranks and titles that have played out their sinister role in Russia, for example, yet continue to signify in present-day Cuba. The Soviet writer Chingiz Aitmatov described it in *Pravda* as follows: "Speaking in plain language, and going to the bottom of things, we must recognize, without euphemism, that we haven't yet eradicated the detrimental implications of the personality cult that seems to have taken over our conscience, our style of work, and our relationships in general. . . . At last, we've freed ourselves from the enforced, pompous formula of publicly introducing a leader with his name preceded by a whole string of positions, titles, degrees, and honorary distinctions."

The Aitmatov statement was prominently published in the June 1987 issue of a Cuban magazine, *Revolución y Cultura*. A writer in Havana commented to me on the importance of having been able to reproduce a text harshly critical of a Communist society. He read aloud a paragraph from the introduction to the Cuban reprint: "The text you're about to read is a clear position regarding the process taking place in present-day Soviet society. What does it mean to live according to the dictates of one's conscience? What should one's civic position be in the context of renewal, democratization, and the dissemination of information? What is meant by social justice?"

I asked him whether it wouldn't be preferable to have a Cuban writer questioned by *Revolución y Cultura* with equal candor on the same subjects.

No, that still wasn't possible, but to have reached the

point where occasionally material such as Aitmatov's can be reproduced implied that a message was being sent on the inevitability of certain changes, that an idea of what was obsolete in Cuba was being provided. He had never thought it would be possible in Castro's lifetime to publish something like that in *Granma,* even translated from Russian. For the time being, that was the only route.

Thus Cuba's problem goes deeper than the deterioration of world economic conditions or the fact that Cuba is in the Caribbean and not on the Black Sea. The problem continues to be the limitations imposed by the impenetrable glass dome on Cubans' lives, their energies, their innermost human nature.

Someone had simplified the subject, I recalled, by stating that *perestroika* changes would likewise take place in Cuba, "with Castro, without Castro, or against Castro." In this person's opinion, however, none of the three possibilities was viable if Castro remained alive for another decade. It would have to be, he added with a smile, through Gorbachev's intervention. He was referring to the $5.6 billion in annual economic aid that Cuba receives from the Soviet Union. But I have the impression that more sinister things than the withdrawal of Soviet aid have been occurring for several years in high government ranks, particularly since July 26, 1980, the twenty-seventh anniversary of the attack on the Moncada barracks, when Haydée Santamaría, who accompanied Fidel Castro during that assault and would remain at Castro's side until her tragic death, committed suicide with a single bullet. I sensed extreme tension during my visit to the offices of *Granma* and in my conversations with Cuban journalists, who balance on a razor's edge, and with one of Castro's intimates from the Sierra Maestra days, who will go unidentified, a person with whom I'm linked in a friendship that has nothing to do with the subject of these notes.

Saul Landau was momentarily distracted while interviewing Fidel Castro. I, too, was distracted, several times, thinking of the end of that "golden legend," as the Castro Revolution was labeled by the writer Regis Debray, Comandante Guevara's comrade among the Bolivian guerrillas. It was a series of executions and assassinations at the top levels of power I was thinking about. The Cubans may be fortunate enough to find a peaceful variant to the changes demanded by the people, which, I am convinced, Cuban leaders fear today more than they do Miami emigrants.

Using Soviet material to advance slightly the opening up of politics and news is a device employed at the moment only by literary magazines and, even among these, in small doses. A Cuban film critic wouldn't dream of demanding a screening of the Soviet film *Repentance.* I had seen it in Madrid, before my arrival in Havana. The only thing the Cubans had been allowed was to reproduce a review from *Literaturnaya Gazeta* by Robert Rozhdestvensky in the January 21, 1987, issue of *La Gaceta,* a monthly published by the Union of Cuban Writers and Artists. I underlined a sentence in the review of this film, which is based on Stalin's paranoid criminal personality. Referring to scandals presumably threatening the Soviet Union, Rozhdestvensky states: "The problem doesn't lie therefore in enemies, but within ourselves." Castroists, inside and outside Cuba, still haven't discovered what is within themselves. It was perhaps such a discovery that led Haydée Santamaría to place the barrel of a .45 inside her mouth and pull the trigger. This wasn't the only suicide of an old comrade. That of ex-president Osvaldo Dorticós was explained as the final escape from a painful illness that had become unbearable.

A group gathered to chat with me on Friday evening, August 21, at the home of the poet Pablo Armando Fernández, editor in chief of *Unión*, a quarterly publication of the Writers Union. They had proposed, through the writer Miguel Barnet, receiving me officially at the Union of Writers and Artists headquarters. I suggested that it would be more intimate to chat at a private home, doing so without an agenda and, above all, without speeches. I'd bring the beverages, whiskey and rum, available to me in dollar stores but unavailable to them. Two bottles of whiskey and two of rum were sufficient, I thought, for ten people. Our hostess served coffee.

In this instance, naming those I spoke to represents no significant danger to them. They are all well attuned to the regime and commit no indiscretions. I had just read a novel by one of them, Jesús Díaz, and although it concerns a Cuban Communist, his achievements and weaknesses, and the trial he is subjected to by his party nucleus or cell, the Soviet example still permeates the text, with episodes from the Great Patriotic War. Something the Russians have already forgotten.

We met in an old, spacious, clean house, although the curtains and more than one piece of furniture were in fairly urgent need of repair. Once, there'd been a garden bordering the sidewalk in front of the house, but now it was totally neglected. The care of gardens and sidewalks is often a task undertaken by dissidents dismissed from their jobs.

Miguel Barnet's international prestige provides him with protection, which he utilizes with prudence and discretion. This most important Cuban writer is a charming, cultivated man, master of a prose style that doesn't seek its roots or models in socialist realism. Of the twentieth century's three best stylists of the Spanish novel in Latin

America, two, in my opinion, are Cuban: Alejo Carpentier and José Lezama Lima (the Mexican Juan Rulfo is the third).

Before meeting at Pablo Armando Fernández's home, Miguel Barnet and I had had dinner at my hotel, El Presidente, but I'd interviewed him previously, at the Hotel Riviera.

A member of an old island family, Barnet was eighteen years old in 1959, the year of the Revolution. He doesn't criticize the Revolution, nor does he write about the Cuba that gave birth to it. He reminded me of Doctor Zhivago, who would have been unable to live outside Russia, whether czarist or Communist. Thus he reminded me of Boris Pasternak. I told him that, and tried to learn when he was going to write about the world around him. Not yet. He still hasn't incorporated it in his innermost being. Anthropologically trained, he needed a lot of distance in time for his themes and characters. I mentioned to him that at the Cuban embassy in Buenos Aires he was identified as a folklorist. He burst out laughing and repeated something he was quoted as saying in an article by the Cuban journalist Alejandro Ríos: "Possibly my ethnological background has contributed to providing me with this deeply rooted point of view. I don't want to talk about anything except Cuba." Some time later I got a copy of the Ríos interview, and this time it was my turn for a hearty laugh, for the journalist's next question was: "How do you explain political commitment in your writing?" He failed to mention Andrei Zhdanov, Stalin's cultural spokesman.

Barnet had remained in Cuba with his family heirlooms, his pets, his memories, and his intimate relationship with the past. Perhaps he had never identified the Revolution with Cuba. In a speech at the publication of his novel *La Vida Real,* he stated: "What we call our country is nothing other than a vast persona embracing us with its trees, mountains, and rivers."

He had managed to slip silently through the cracks he found or invented during the time of the repression of homosexuals, the period when a writer was supposed to be "an engineer of the soul," as Stalinist theology put it. In this country, as recently as 1987, Armando Hart, the minister of culture and a veteran of the Sierra Maestra, quoted a text by Anatoly Lunacharsky, Lenin's commissar of culture, at a Forum of Literary Criticism and Research, thereby indicating to the group what the Revolution expected of them. As for himself, Hart added: "In art and culture one must move toward processes of greater participation and democracy, but this is guaranteed only when it is based on high social responsibility." The degree of one's "social responsibility"—a pseudoscientific formula invoked to avoid mentioning party discipline or flattery— is what determines who gets published, who has access to newspaper publication, who speaks on radio or television, who travels to congresses abroad, who can return from abroad with a television set or an air conditioner.

In 1967, shortly after Barnet reached the age of twenty-six, his novel *Biography of a Runaway Slave* was published, and ever since he has been the most important Cuban figure in contemporary Spanish literature.

He has enough irony, suppleness, and control of the language to engage in dialogue without either defending or attacking the Revolution or El Comandante. He is not a dissident, but an intellectual linked to a world that extends far beyond the Revolution and its Comandante, and he's organized things so as not to disturb that world. He said as much in his speech: "I've gone beyond historical truth to something I feel is much more real: credibility. In so doing, I don't think I've hurt the social history of my country." El Comandante couldn't demand that he include the Revolution in that credibility. Yes, Barnet has his world within arm's reach in Cuba, he breathes it, he strokes it. He does not wish to disturb his creativity or divide himself with the unremitting effort of an exile.

He does belong to the Writers Union, and attends international meetings of intellectuals and artists organized by the regime; but he never makes speeches on Internationalism and Literature, Art and Revolution, the Latin American Theme; nor does he thank the Revolution for the opportunity of writing, publishing, and uniting with the people; nor is he one of the regime's official spokesmen, who still invoke the Soviet writers Fyodor Gladkov and Mikhail Sholokhov. He attends foreign book fairs when invited, but doesn't rack himself over intrigues erupting at the Writers Union when official delegations are chosen. He complains bitterly about the shortage of books to read, is unfamiliar with much of contemporary literature, particularly German literature translated and published in Spain, and has meager information about what's going on in the world. But he doesn't need all that for his own writing. All he needs is Cuba.

He criticizes the official policy of taking over his foreign rights, and hopes to raise the subject at the next writers' meeting with El Comandante. How would he do it? I ask. He considers himself an expert in guessing at Fidel Castro's mood, and El Comandante is very lenient when in a good mood. The last time the writers had a meeting with Fidel, Barnet didn't feel it was the right moment.

He's a very witty and fluent talker; as we're having dinner, the pianist in the hotel dining room dedicates some songs to him. The hotel was built by one of his forebears, who was briefly chief of state. Barnet toys with his

sses a lot, putting them on and taking them off, an
winds up trying on mine.

Though he goes along with the regime's required rituals, his personality is a lively exercise in spontaneity. He
doesn't scrutinize me, nor is he guarded, two barriers that
have frustrated many of my dialogues on the island. One
of the rituals starts tomorrow in Managua, where he'll
be presiding over a literary jury. He will be departing
shortly, which doesn't please him, and is fully aware of the
difficulties that will have to be surmounted in order for
him to survive two or three days in Nicaragua, but he's
glad to have collected toothpaste, soap, razor blades, toilet
paper, to bring to his friends.

Barnet isn't familiar with the Nicaraguan poet Juan
Chow. I discuss this unknown writer, whose poetry I'd
come across accidentally two years earlier in Managua. I
had wanted to meet him, and one day he showed up at my
hotel at noon. Though very slight, almost a dwarf, he de-
voured a huge lunch. I had discovered a couple of his
poems in a magazine but hadn't been able to find any
books by him. He was employed in the Sandinista association of cultural workers, and although one of his books had
been approved, he was waiting for paper, which was
strictly rationed, to become available, so it could be sent
to press. Barnet doesn't respond when I mention that in
Managua Juan Chow's boss, Rosario Murillo, President
Daniel Ortega's wife, gave me a new book of her poems,
which had been very well received: a true poet.

Juan Chow, through mysterious forking paths, as Jorge
Luis Borges would put it, was a great admirer of the
French poet St. John Perse and of Borges himself. He had
read them both in borrowed books and had Xerox copies
of their writings. Barnet had no intention of offering Juan
Chow his own editions of Perse and Borges. I never

earned what happened to Juan Chow, a great Nicaraguan poet.

As for Miguel Barnet, a Florentine spirit who has to inhabit, without impassioned participation, the island of the Castro Revolution, he maintains neutrality.

Late at night, I made some notes of our conversation. I reproduce them here just as they appear in my notebook, without claiming them to be verbatim. But this, more or less, is how Miguel Barnet replied to the questions I asked:

"If Kafka were writing in Cuba, would he be able to publish here?"

"Maybe not, but he could publish abroad. After all, he wrote in Prague and didn't care to publish everything."

"But if he published only abroad, could he live in Cuba without being criticized?"

"Before, not; now, possibly."

"Would he be persecuted?"

"No. He'd certainly be criticized by the official press— and everything is official—though if someone prestigious defended him, he'd be protected from reprisals."

"Someone from Cuba or from abroad?"

"Preferably from abroad. Besides, many writers in the capitalist world had a hard time, particularly James Joyce and D. H. Lawrence."

"Supposing he wanted to leave the country?"

"Many high officials would be opposed to it, but Fidel would decide in his favor."

I call Barnet's attention to the delicate balance of his replies, whereas his books leave no human passion unraveled. He smiles. And recalls something he said recently in a speech: "Celestial Aquarius beneath victorious Uranus, with a shower of stars on the palm of my right hand."

Keeping a delicate balance myself with regard to various subjects, I manage to incorporate into the dialogue the subject of the work camps, the so-called reeducation

camps, where homosexuals were imprisoned. I men
that in the early seventies, at the height of homosex
repression, I sent a journalist to Havana and published
series of his comments on Cuba in my newspaper. These
were highly favorable toward the Revolution. Enrique
Raab was a brilliant writer, and the series was subsequently published as a book; but Raab, who was homosexual, wrote nothing about those matters. I add that Raab,
an only child of Holocaust survivors, was kidnapped under
the Argentine dictatorship and is one more among the
disappeared.

This tack doesn't get me far. Barnet believes that something was done about that repression, and he mentions a
letter from the Writers Union to Fidel Castro. But why,
twenty years after the fall of fascism in Italy, should the
Castro regime have conceived of imposing on homosexuals the same system of "reeducation" that Benito Mussolini applied in his country? And do so not in a backward,
Catholic nation like Italy in the thirties but in a permissive
society like that of Cuba in the seventies, at a time when
countless homosexuals around the world were wearing
T-shirts with Che Guevara's face painted on the chest.

These are, I realize, not the sort of questions you ask a
refugee from the world of ethnography. He isn't annoyed.
I then summarize the version given me by a mutual colleague, and mention that I'm not interested in the statistics on who and how many individuals were reeducated.
I want to know how he, Barnet, views the mentality of
those who conceived these abuses, thinking they were
doing the Revolution a service.

Taking out my notebook, I read in a low voice:

" 'The problem of homosexuals was always linked in
revolutionary morality and political analysis to the relations existing between prostitution and corruption as controlled by the U.S. East Coast Mafia. At first only prosti-

s were reeducated, but this caused the leaders to think t homosexuality was also correctible through reeduca- on. There's a great deal of ignorance and a certain amount of machismo among the leaders, who were afraid of the hippie revolt of the sixties. The Revolution still hadn't succeeded in creating developmental structures for Cuban youths who had lived in a climate of prostitu- tion created by the United States Mafia. There were two years of persecutions organized by a minister subse- quently accused of being a repressed homosexual. Homo- sexuals were arrested in the streets, seized from their homes, and sent to reeducation camps. Even those who had stopped living as homosexuals and had well-estab- lished families were tried. Informing and the corruption produced by informing surfaced: obtaining a place to live or a job promotion, getting even with someone, envy, jealousy, not to mention getting a divorce in a society where a Communist whose wife was unfaithful might find himself charged with unrevolutionary conduct. These men were humiliated, handled roughly.' "

I pause in my reading and tell Barnet that I had a dai- quiri one day at the Floridita bar with a Cuban journalist, a homosexual art critic working at the time for the intelli- gence services. Two couples went by and insulted me in a low voice. The man isn't a friend of Barnet's, but he knows him.

I ask Barnet if I could get a copy of the proceedings of one of those homosexual trials. He assumes that all have been burned. Perhaps someone has kept a copy? He knows of no one. He thinks Fidel Castro had a lot to do with ending that era, a black page in Cuban history, but such times of shame exist in all countries. He thinks El Comandante was unaware of what was going on.

This isn't the first time I have encountered this re- sponse. Time and again, El Comandante appears as a strange being whose never-sleeping, penetrating eyes, focused on Cuba, can discern a school in bad condition in remote Chivirico on the southern coast, but fail to see the work camps and never read a declaration signed in Paris, New York, and Madrid petitioning for the freedom of some homosexual intellectual.

That's as far as Miguel Barnet allowed himself to go. Beyond that meant entering the realm of hypocrisy. For one doesn't play around with El Comandante. And thus, seated in the hotel dining room, unable to gaze into Fidel Castro's eyes to guess his mood, what else was Miguel Barnet supposed to say?

Barnet drove ahead in his car to guide me to Pablo Armando Fernández's home. In the long evening that followed, there were several difficult moments. It was one year after Fidel Castro had decided to revert to the economic restrictions of 1960, thereby blocking the path toward an opening up that had begun in the early eighties. This regression not only created a shortage of market goods, especially food, but seriously aggravated the already harrowing housing problem. Corruption was inevitable, and the struggle to obtain political positions that brought certain privileges was ruthless.

Exactly one year before, in 1986, the private sale of dwellings was again prohibited. I visited a friend, a professor of architecture who had to continue to live with his wife several years after an unpleasant divorce, until finally he was able to get hold of some material to erect a divider. Officially he was the guest of the owner of the house.

My 1987 meeting with the writers took place at a time when Fidel Castro was obsessed with the changes just then beginning in Eastern European countries, especially the Soviet Union. His reaction to those policies that gave the socialist revolution a new character was a reversion to revolutionary purity, consumer sacrifice, voluntary non-remunerative work. The search for allies led him to Kim Il Sung, and North Korean achievements were praised to the skies in the communications media. As the Harvard political scientist Jorge I. Domínguez concisely summed things up in *Foreign Affairs:* "Unlike the Soviet Union, most of Eastern Europe, and certainly China, Cuba may be the first Communist regime in the late 1980s to back off from market mechanisms in order to improve production and efficiency." In any event, I have the impression that Castro was addressing a kind of cultural revolution rather than simply an economic problem.

For Cubans, who must remain within the political framework of the regime in order to survive with minimal decency, the imposition of this absolutist revolutionary line made it impossible, however deftly modulated it was by writers, to hold any enriched or nuanced dialogue.

An obligatory subject was the misery in which the Cuban population lived—the collective impossibility of satisfying minimal needs. The inevitable answer which I'd previously received time and again and was likewise thrown at me that night placed the blame for shortages on the U.S. imperialist blockade. Though I'm convinced that it would favor specific U.S. interests to establish normal relations with Cuba and not to interfere in its internal affairs, I couldn't believe that a country able to trade with almost the entire world with the sole exception, among the great powers, of the United States, is incapable of organizing its economy and enabling its fertile soil, which receives generous rainfall, to produce food. Besides, I refused to accept the Cubans' concept of being fenced in or blockaded. Cuba was not fenced in or blockaded; its channels of communication to other countries were all open.

The writers came prepared. They cited the case of an Argentine developer who had decided to build a dozen hotels in Cuba, to absorb future tourism. The private bank that had agreed to finance the operation, they said, backed out of the deal as the result of U.S. pressure.

It was a comical moment. For as they were arguing about this aspect of the economic blockade, Barnet kept signaling them to be still, until finally he interrupted them. During our dinner earlier, Barnet had cited this same example when I asked him to explain how the blockade worked.

I was familiar with the incident, which was public knowledge in Buenos Aires. The Argentine developer didn't have the personal wherewithal to provide the capital funds, and Cuba didn't possess the funds at that time. He sought financing from the Argentine government within the framework of its policy to promote its exports. Thus, if Cuba failed to meet its payments, the loss would be absorbed by Buenos Aires. But the fact is that Cuba had interrupted payments on its existing debt for exports received from Argentina, and the Argentine government refused to increase the Cuban debt.

An anecdote on this debt appeared in a book on President Raúl Alfonsín, by the journalist Pablo Giussani, who asks: "Your visit to Cuba took place soon after a congress opposed to payment of foreign debt convened there, didn't it?"

"Yes," replies Alfonsín. "By the way, I told Fidel Castro jokingly that the international congress against the payment of the foreign debt was geared toward allowing Cuba not to pay Argentina. It so happens that Cuba owed us some funds, and I remember now, in connection with this matter, an episode we laughingly talked about in Havana with Vice-President Carlos Rafael Rodríguez. When the head of the Central Bank of Cuba went to Buenos Aires to inform us of a postponement of payment, I replied: 'We were too many, and Grandma gave birth.' The vice-president informed me afterward, during my visit, that the president of the Central Bank had transmitted my reaction literally, leaving everyone rather perplexed, for they didn't know what I actually meant. Rodríguez, a participant in the meeting, intervened at that point, he told me, to explain that this humorous expression, fairly common usage in Spain as well as in Argentina, expressed the utter deterioration of a particular situation."

Cuban writers weren't informed of the debt to Argentina and were unaware that Argentina was, at that time, the island's principal Latin American commercial partner.

The group could give me no other examples of how the economic blockade worked. In turn I claimed that much more serious than the third-world countries' inability to export industrial products containing Cuban nickel to the United States was the closing of the free fruit and vegetable markets, which had allowed farmers to sell what they produced above and beyond the compulsory quota given the government. El Comandante refused to permit the existence of these nouveaux riches and to allow farmers to benefit from other sectors of the economy, but the fact is that thanks to them Cubans were able to eat better.

Raúl Alfonsín's joke to Castro about the international congress's opposition to foreign debt reflected something more than irony. This congress was a festival of economists, artists, and journalists, and there arose grave suspicions that the purpose of the event, which was totally financed by Cuba, including fare and hotel (I turned down an invitation to attend as a journalist), was to find a role for Fidel Castro in Latin America and to create a political cover-up for the pressing need of postponing payments to Cuba's creditors.

Castro didn't want to admit or allow to be admitted what was self-evident: His theory that rich Communist countries must finance their poor Communist brethren was falling apart. Likewise crumbling was his strategy of obtaining economic support from the new democracies that have sprung up in Latin America in the last decade. He adhered to the German Democratic Republic and was pursuing North Korea, where Communist banners were still waving.

In August 1987, the full text of Mikhail Gorbachev's Report to the Joint Session of the Central Committee, held in January 1987, was still undisclosed. I sent one of the writers the copy I'd brought with me to Havana, published in Spanish in Buenos Aires. I'd underlined a paragraph: "The theoretical notions of socialism remained, in many respects, at the level of the thirties and forties, when society had completely different tasks." Something similar happened to me on my second visit to Nicaragua, in 1985, with regard to the revolutionaries' ignorance of what truly was taking place in the Soviet Union. I made the trip from New York and brought with me several copies of a recent issue of *Time* magazine, which contained a long article on Gorbachev. The article was studied carefully, for never had the Nicaraguans held in their hands such complete, candid material on Gorbachev's ideas; but the Sandinista leaders continued to look toward Cuba, whose language, symbols, and gestures they understood.

Other difficult moments of dialogue sprang more than anything from total ignorance about world events on the part of the Cuban intellectuals assembled that evening. On the one hand, they had no access to news. Mainly, however, having access to news meant entering a dangerous area that entailed comparison with the party line, and deviating from the party line meant inevitable entry into marginality.

Two young writers on the staff of *La Gaceta* burst out laughing when I defined myself as a Socialist-Zionist.

Their notion of the Middle Eastern conflict was determined by fundamentalist Arab views, primarily those of the Libyans. They were unaware of the new approaches of the PLO and certainly knew nothing about the existence of pacifist organizations in Israel, or of the meetings between members of these groups and Yasir Arafat or his collaborators.

The subject of Judaism didn't come up in the conversation. No one harasses Jews living in Cuba; the Jewish theme is nonexistent, nor is there any notion of the intellectual richness Judaism has contributed to contemporary culture. When our host took me to the door, he mentioned that his family was of Jewish origin. Barnet, too, thought that he was of Sephardic descent. But in both instances this was mentioned almost casually, when we were alone. It would have been more natural to hear it during our group conversation.

Before visiting Cuba, I hung a chain on my neck with a prominently visible Star of David. Often in conversation I'd toy with the chain, taking it out of my shirt. At the beach, you couldn't help noticing it. My intention was to observe the reactions this produced. Which were: None. Never, at any moment, did a Cuban make a remark about it or ask a question. This may seem normal in an open, pluralistic country; but in Cuba, where everything one says or asks can be compromising, it appeared evident to me once more that spontaneity of facial expression isn't matched by that of words. Cubans are verbally immobilized. Frozen.

I expressed my surprise that postrevolutionary Cuba, in existence now for almost thirty years, has not produced a literature. This gap, in my opinion, didn't stem from a lack of freedom of expression, from censorship, or from the uprooting effect of exile. But rather, I thought, it was due to a dearth of writers who felt no automatic obligation or compulsion to identify everything with the present, when in fact certain things pertained to a much vaster realm: the human condition. What was needed was one generation, or perhaps a single writer, who didn't equate the Cuban hell and the hell of exile within a schematic, political framework. Or who proposed and succeeded in initiating a dialogue between the "two Cubas," omitting political confrontation. Intellectuals should be capable of shifting back and forth naturally between the island of Cuba and Cuba-in-exile—that is, naturally regarding the conflict as one more, just one more, of the elements constituting a nation and a culture, not as a battle in which one of the two sides had to be destroyed. I cited Saint-Just, Robespierre's disciple, who thought the only way to build the republic was by "destruction of everything opposing it."

There had been many attempts at dialogue between the two shores, even meetings between important delegations of exiled Cubans and revolutionary authorities in Havana to resolve problems of separated families, financial aid to relatives in Cuba, the freeing of political prisoners. But the basic theme was missing: defining what Cuba was as a whole.

The efforts of the editors of *Areíto,* a magazine published in New York, were considerable. One of them, Carlos Muñiz Varela, was killed in Costa Rica by anti-Castro Cubans. In 1984, in *Areíto*'s special tenth-anniversary issue, Jorge I. Domínguez pointed out in his appraisal of Cubans in exile:

> The emigration theory has been clearly linked, through the years, with liberal political philosophy. It is the individual, at a particular juncture, who decides not to collaborate or submit to the society he had hitherto belonged to. . . . Many left Cuba simply

because they were affected economically. But this doesn't prevent émigrés from sharing a common moral background: all objected to the monopoly of action on the part of the revolutionary government and claimed their right to a more pluralistic system that allowed free economic, social, political, and religious competition.

Although relationships between Cubans on the island and those in Miami ceased being exclusively terroristic or insulting some time ago—the term *gusanos* (worms) to designate those in exile has disappeared from the Cuban press—the writers I spoke to refused to accept my conviction that the Cuban identity of the refugees in the United States was more vigorous and dynamic than what I had encountered in Cuba itself. Cuban literature in the best Cuban tradition, I concluded, would emerge in Miami or New York sooner than in Cuba itself. And it would emerge not as a political position evolving from the field of culture but as a non-Manichean understanding of Cuban identity, in which Castro's Revolution was not the most significant event.

True blasphemy.

Perhaps it was unfair of me to have imagined in their presence the place and context for the burgeoning Cuban novel. I should have speculated that someone in our present company, even the Stalinist Jesús Díaz, might be writing it at that very moment, either in his inner being, the words imprinted solely in memory, or in some isolated corner of his house, during lone, anguished hours: like poems and novels memorized by political prisoners in Soviet jails.

They responded vigorously to my blasphemy. The response was largely self-directed, with the classic arguments regarding a writer's role in a revolutionary society: remarks reiterated through the years, translated from Soviet terminology of the fundamentalist period into fluent Caribbean Spanish.

It was a reiteration of the debate already raging at the tables of progressive intellectuals swept away by the gale of news from Communist countries. The experience of these regimes in the last half century is very explicit with regard to the mirages generally regulating revolutionary, cultural roles.

The writers were on a dead-end street, were crushed and immobilized by a twenty-five-year-old tombstone. A quarter of a century had elapsed since the great assembly of Cuban writers and the political leadership: Fidel Castro, Carlos Rafael Rodríguez, Osvaldo Dorticós. Twenty-five years in a great vacuum since that debate in the National Library regarding the themes and attitudes that Cuban writers ought to take, explore, and project within the revolutionary framework. A meeting imbued with fear, doubts, illusions, intrigues and accusations, hopes.

By August 1987, the boldest and best had either died or departed into exile after having endured betrayals and persecutions from the very individuals drinking rum with me now.

José Lezama Lima had died. Though he never possessed the combative impulses to dare to defend freedom of expression, his voluminous physical and spiritual presence served as a reference point in appraising the universality of culture.

Alejo Carpentier had died. During his lifetime he maintained an almost complicit silence with political power. The official culture could extrapolate material from his speeches, interviews, and lectures to deify the Revolution, to endow it with a civilized patina and intellectuality. But refuge could also be found in a different reading of Carpentier's work, which for many served as an ancillary lung to prevent suffocation, or as consolation.

In an article on Leo Tolstoy's significance for Latin America, Carpentier recommends that Cuban writers use the model of *War and Peace* for recounting the events that occurred on the revolutionary island: "What interested me, in this instance, was the method applied by the Russian novelist in a work that reconstructed events, then presented them with *utter freedom.*"

Alejo Carpentier emerged from surrealism; he wrote extensively in French; his hermetic, baroque novels were virtually incomprehensible to the Cuban public. In his own way, he served everyone, including the government, through his uncritical loyalty to Castroism. But because he enjoyed broad thematic freedom, the entire development of modern culture surfaced in his writings and lectures. He was an open window—the only one, I believe, in Castro's Cuba—to the artistic vanguards of the twentieth century. Sixteen years after the Revolution, in the "Year of the First Congress of the Communist Party of Cuba," 1975, he was unafraid to explain the journalist's role, citing Victor Hugo, Émile Zola, and Anatole France, not mentioning once, throughout his speech, the Cuban or the Soviet press.

Curiously, it was the French surrealist poet Robert Desnos—killed by the Nazis in Terezin concentration camp, shortly before the camp was liberated in 1945 by Soviet troops en route to Berlin—who managed while passing through Havana in 1928 to free the likewise surrealist Carpentier from the jails of the dictator Gerardo Machado.

No other writer in Castro's Cuba would speak, as Carpentier did, of a reality beyond the real, quoting Guillaume Apollinaire's "the beauty of the real that is more real than the real" and adding: "that is, the reality hidden behind everyday observed reality." This indeed was a blasphemy against socialist realism, a demolition of the theology imposed from the upper political echelons, which held that nothing was more real and evident than the reality presented in the party line.

For a quarter of a century, one could read Alejo Carpentier between the lines and ignore his political opinions, his obsequiousness toward the regime. But to have incorporated that into his writing meant organizing a dual existence. No one else was granted by the regime the extrapolated cultural freedom enjoyed by Carpentier. In the decade since his death, that place has remained vacant. Meanwhile, Heberto Padilla, Guillermo Cabrera Infante, Carlos Franqui, and Severo Sarduy found themselves forced to leave the country.

Padilla got out of Havana through García Márquez, just as Carpentier managed to escape the island through the intervention of Robert Desnos. In Cuba, history always repeats itself as tragedy. What could I expect from these writers who had been entrusted with the task of holding a discussion with me? Even if they didn't deviate from the party line in what they wrote and published, their mere desire to agree to read contemporary literature was in itself a challenge to the regime, a confrontation with those who decreed the official aesthetic of the Revolution.

Writers have sons in the army, families to feed, the need to improve their housing, obtain spare parts for dilapidated cars, be able to publish. Everything depends on the state, and even in the year 1987, an accusation or observation from the critic and writer Agenor Martí in *Granma* could terminate a career, force someone to leave a university position, thrust a writer into nothingness. Agenor Martí himself in 1979 hailed the vigor of the Cuban detective novel, which had emerged eight years before. This abominable text of his was reprinted without the slightest change in 1983, as if it were an official document, when a collection of detective stories was published. In one single paragraph he liquidates the detective novel whose investigators are concerned with bourgeois legality: Sherlock Holmes, Hercule Poirot, Maigret, Perry Mason. And he goes on to add that in the Cuban detective novel, "a new, essential aspect in the whole history of the genre always emerges: the action of the people grouped together in their mass organizations, mainly in the Committees for the Defense of the Revolution."

To some extent Martí was right. A new kind of detective novel appeared in Cuba: one that promoted informing.

Actually, I didn't care to win an argument that evening. If I provoked them, it was simply to gain some understanding of how they felt, how they thought. They presented themselves as ideologues and revolutionaries, and I was prepared to accept them as such, providing that something of their own lives surfaced, giving some indication of their inner selves, the inevitable tragedies of the creative individual under any regime in any situation.

Harmonious lives, unquestioned convictions, in revolutionary Cuba? I don't believe it. Nor did I believe it that evening, weaving in and out among different topics and nostalgic notions. The writers were defending all they had left: the possibility of survival.

In the prologue to *Heroes Graze in My Garden,* the exiled Heberto Padilla comments on this novel, which he wrote in Cuba: "The fate of each of these characters, the situations they're involved in, are inconclusive, because everything you write about in an asphyxiating political atmosphere is inconclusive and fragmentary."

That evening I had with me a group of fragmented, inconclusive characters. I'm waiting, expectantly, to see them again after Castro is gone, when they themselves can comb through newspapers and magazines of the fifties and discover that Batista's defeat was achieved in the cities of the plains, in student and workers' strikes, and not in the Sierra Maestra; when they are able to reread the publications of the three decades following the night that Fulgencio Batista escaped from the island, and thereby confirm the degradation they have been subjected to. In order to be able, perhaps, to reread their own writings and rewrite them, using the same material but feeling free to organize it spontaneously, fearlessly.

They will have to recall Alejo Carpentier's advice but read it differently, probing the true inner meanings that Carpentier's vast culture ascribed to them. This is included in the article by Carpentier on Tolstoy's method in writing *War and Peace,* an article published in Moscow in 1961 and in Havana twenty-six years later, an incredible lapse considering that it's addressed to Cuban writers. Carpentier extolled: "a method that consisted in utilizing any available document that nurtured his thirst for information about the period he was interested in. We know the role played by his research into memoirs and notebooks, firsthand accounts, diplomatic correspondence and oral history, in the development of his novel, which contains entire paragraphs out of Thiers. That is the only way an epic novel is produced. And if the Cuban Revolution, sooner or later, is to be interpreted in terms of an epic novel, it will be fruitful for the author to reflect on the research methods and methods of expression employed by Leo Tolstoy in writing *War and Peace,* a work alongside which others, purportedly historic, strike us as false and decrepit, both in essence and in form."

To expect Tolstoy's dedication in the researching methods of Cuban writers was somewhat excessive. Cuba had been at war in Angola for twelve years; hundreds of thousands of Cubans must have participated in that carnage, as well as in Ethiopia. For writers, the subject of war was reduced to a political matter, which failed to inspire them as men of culture. The long war had not stirred a thematic revolution, a revision of values, an emotional upheaval.

It is impossible for a society to undergo years of war without its literature requiring an expression of the great themes of death and fear. Twelve years of war, and there is no war literature, not one novel or poem that goes beyond pamphleteering stupidity. Not one inch further. The explanation I received, that this literature hasn't appeared because no Cuban writer would ever jeopardize Angola's freedom with his revelations, was too much even for someone coming, as I do, from a country where Eva Perón had been officially declared "Spiritual Leader of the Nation."

Fortunately, a few days later I found some relief from this smug, stultifying atmosphere of official intellectualism, through a visit from a young dissident journalist. We sat on the terrace of the Hotel Presidente, which covers the entire corner of Avenida de los Presidentes and Calle 7, two hundred yards from the sea.

Rolando Cartaya arrived loaded with documents: articles he'd written for the evening newspaper *Juventud Rebelde,* amusing accounts of his current profession of spraying private gardens, records of his dismissal from the newspaper, his trial, prison. He hoped to be allowed to leave Cuba, and I think that he finally succeeded. But Cartaya's real story, I believe, is to be found elsewhere: in the meaning of that routine episode of a journalist criticized for an article and losing his job in order not to surrender his dignity.

I read around ten of his pieces, most of which deal with cultural themes. An excellent review of a Vivaldi concert, interviews with musicians and contemporary interpreters such as the Italian Luigi Nono, the Brazilian Chico

Buarque, the Argentine Nacha Guevara, and the Cuban Silvio Rodríguez.

In all his articles, Cartaya reveals an exquisite sensibility, a true affinity for his themes, taking an emotional stand, using rich, fertile language that goes beyond the limitations imposed by repetitious political slogans. But he doesn't stray from official ideology. His future as a journalist, and perhaps as a writer, was assured in Cuba.

One of his articles begins as follows: "One of the distinctive characteristics in Silvio Rodríguez's work—determined by the author's personality, which in turn has been conditioned by experiences amid the Revolution—is the presence of dialectics. Immersed in a historic moment of multiple antagonisms, ranging from confrontation between coexisting social systems to the sometimes agonizing processes experienced by the individual in a phase of radical changes, the troubadour always aims in his songs toward an infusion of that struggle of opposites which gives a definite sense of historical process."

Nothing the official censors could object to.

In a review of the song "Soy Snob" (I'm a Snob) by Nacha Guevara, with lyrics by the French musician Boris Vian, Cartaya wrote: "Snobbism is a social by-product generated in capitalism by the cultural industry. The mass media draw the attention of a mass population with limited economic power to a range of standards of behavior, style, and priorities that are unattainable, or, at best, untenable: models veering from extravagant to superfluous and forming part of the phenomenon of rising expectations, of the dream mechanism that secures the establishment and simultaneously produces super-earnings."

Nothing objectionable.

Rolando Cartaya is young, has a good job, a place to live, a family, a revolution, and he has Fidel.

And one day, by chance, he attends another performance: the police repression of a group of Cubans trying to seek asylum in a Latin American embassy. Cartaya was politically prepared to avow that no Cuban ought to abandon the Revolution. He was in wholehearted agreement that these uprooted, marginal Cubans should be prevented from taking asylum in an embassy. But something broke inside Cartaya when he was confronted with the ferocity of political repression: the bloody beating to which defenseless men, women, and children were subjected; the gratuitous repression of a group that posed no threat to the police.

He wrote his article, which was rejected at *Juventud Rebelde,* along with a serious warning. Some time later, he had it sent to an international news agency—and this was the "crime" for which he was tried and convicted.

He didn't take back his words when he lost his job, when he was persecuted, when food was scarce at home. Which is why I think that Cartaya's real story must be the one detailing the inner path of his feelings and ideas, which incited this sudden, dizzying act of conscience.

Cartaya explains it in his own way. He was reared a Catholic: a reflex act of Christian piety toward one's neighbor. I remind him that I myself am from a country where almost all the Catholic bishops supported and blessed the torturers and murderers of a military dictatorship, encouraged and justified them; a country where torturers and murderers were likewise Catholic.

Besides, an act of piety differs from taking a defiant stand, for the latter results in a bold act. An act of piety can be limited merely to a silent moral crisis. The great majority of Cubans, after all, are undergoing a silent, uncommitted crisis of conscience. Rolando Cartaya went beyond that.

And that's what is hard to capture in Cubans. They have

internalized their fear of the regime in such a way that seldom will they say that the regime itself is what must totally change. And, even further, that it must disappear, collapse. It is almost impossible for them to give free rein to that normal human desire for everything to end at one stroke, for having everything change radically. They were saying this before Fulgencio Batista's flight, in the final year of struggle: Let the damned year of 1958 end once and for all. At present, the boundary that Cubans do not cross is the territory occupied by El Comandante and his regime.

The second time we meet, Cartaya brings me a letter that I asked him to write to organizations defending freedom of expression, particularly to Peter Galliner, director of the International Press Institute, who promptly became involved in the case by protesting against the Cuban government. Cartaya has meager writing materials at his disposal, and I give him some of the notebooks and pens that I brought in quantity for my research.

But still I'm unable to decipher the geography of his decision: how to place oneself in Cartaya's universe? The religious explanation is inconclusive in a country where religion is merely a varnish for pre-Christian myths and beliefs, which are more mysterious, binding, unattainable, musical, and sensual in their hold.

My reason for dwelling on this unknown quality in relation to Cartaya is that herein may lie the key to what will suddenly, inevitably, occur in Cuba: the collapse of the Castro Revolution. Will it break at the top? Will it explode at the bottom? What sorts of hidden movements are taking place in the Cuban spirit? That hidden anxiety which still hasn't reached impossible limits, which isn't erupting within the corridors of the regime. What's going on deep inside of Cubans who decide to take a stand on a few small things and disregard all the rest, patiently surviving on food lines, taking refuge in music and dance, in sensuality, in the warm weather, in the sea?

Being with Cartaya is pleasant. His conversation is free of sanctimonious declamation, that infernal racket employed by the regime to confuse Cubans and beguile many foreign observers.

He's a curious, well-bred young man who decided without any malice or egotism to grapple with something that suddenly befell him. I'm touched by his continued loyalty after the terrible injustice he happened to experience. But in order to get a clear answer to my questions, it will be necessary, no doubt, to wait for the Cuban people to raise these questions on their own and answer them for themselves.

I listen to Cartaya in silence, with that attitude described by someone he himself once interviewed, Luigi Nono: "Silence serves to listen to what is not understood, the pulse of blood in our veins, our haziest memories, the diversity of world cultures."

I thought of Rolando Cartaya more than once. It was after all better to be a fumigator without steady work than a journalist on *Juventud Rebelde.* Unexpected alternatives: poisoning garden insects or Cuban minds. The subject of written journalism was also of concern to Fidel Castro at that time, but without the courage displayed by Cartaya. There was a joke attributed to Castro: "Rainy days double the sale of *Granma,* owing to the umbrella shortage." A year before, in May 1986, El Comandante had summoned a meeting of the most prestigious Cuban journalists to analyze the press situation; its utter lack of credibility rendered the press useless as an instrument of the Revolution. For twenty uninterrupted hours, in the best Castro style, they listened, they discussed, and—according to the account given some months later by Lázaro

Barredo, ex–managing editor of *Juventud Rebelde* and currently vice-president of the Journalists Union of Cuba—they reached the conclusion that "the chief problems facing our press stemmed from two phenomena: the mystery syndrome and the suppression mentality." One could come to that conclusion simply by glancing at a Cuban newspaper, without having to exchange opinions with the chief of state for twenty hours. Or to endure thirty years of revolution.

Still another year went by. In June 1987, Lázaro Barredo explained in the Argentine weekly *El Periodista* that, thanks to the earlier decisions, "the Cuban press will cease being compliant and slogan-ridden, and become a decisive tool not only for extolling the Revolution's achievements but, in addition, for criticizing abuses of power, underutilization of resources, and bureaucratic red tape."

A few weeks later, I arrived in Havana and had dinner at the home of a journalist from Agence France Presse, together with Enrique Román, the newly appointed editor in chief of *Granma,* who assumed this high position in order to implement changes in accordance with the famous meeting. The chief columnist of the newspaper, Luis Báez, was also there.

In my forty years as a journalist, I've observed many dichotomies, but none with such a chasm as separated the daily matter of *Granma* from the plans put forth to me by its editor in chief. Enrique Román had decided to travel to Europe, where he would examine from the inside the functioning of large newspapers, particularly *El País* of Madrid and *La Repubblica* of Rome. The fact that he preferred these huge, democratic newspapers of capitalist societies to the formulaic *Pravda* seemed like an enormous qualitative leap, though I told him that the chief problem affecting *Granma* could be resolved without leaving Havana, by just imitating *Pravda*'s present-day attitudes. In Cuba these days, however, looking to the Soviets for inspiration is virtually synonymous with treason and anti-Castroism.

All Román would have had to do was open the pages of *Granma* to national and international news, as had been done with *El País* and *La Repubblica,* without feeling bound to anything other than the editors' own professional judgment and intuition. The key to the success of both those newspapers was in the openness of their news coverage and not in their internal organization or utilization of modern machinery.

As always, it proved impossible to conduct this kind of conversation with a government official. The focus quickly shifted, as in the writers' meeting, to the role one should play in a revolutionary process—in this instance, the journalist's role. There was no room for the concept of calling or profession.

We returned time and again to the subject of roles. If a journalist's obligation or aspiration was to create a Marxist, revolutionary press, why be concerned with the quality or efficiency of the journalism he practiced? Nothing he could learn in Western Europe would be of use to him, since any positive modification of *Granma* must begin with an opening up, however slight, of its news coverage. The people I was speaking to refused to acknowledge that journalism was something totally alien to the society they lived in and wished to perpetuate. They had no need of journalism, and no need to look for it, I told them. It was a less mysterious profession than they thought, with no inaccessible secrets, but it required a different political context. Capitalistic journalism, they imagined, had access to some peculiar mechanism whereby Marxism could be taught and nonexistent victories could be proclaimed in such a way as to whet the reader's interest and assure credibility.

I proposed that we work together on a single issue of *Granma,* and in just twenty-four hours they would be able to verify the change that would take place. There was logic in the answer they gave me: the experience would last for only one day. We all laughed. But, as I added, what a day in the history of journalism!

They showed sincere concern about improving the Cuban press and sought some formula to pave the way for the liberalizing of news coverage. There were lots of jokes about their duties, and someone remarked that newspaper circulation would drop when there was adequate production of plastic bags for household garbage. And once again, as in almost all conversation with members of the regime, the name of the man most mentioned after Fidel Castro came up. They said that García Márquez had told El Comandante he couldn't live in Cuba on a permanent basis because it was essential for him to read the newspaper over breakfast every morning, and there were no newspapers in Cuba. Nonetheless, he was given a protocol house and frequently resides there.

During my interview with Carlos Rafael Rodríguez, he revealed that he, too, was concerned about the poor quality of the press. More than a year after that marathon meeting with El Comandante, the initiatives for reducing the space given to ideology and providing more space for reality had been confined to appointing a new editor in chief of *Granma,* authorizing coverage of police reporting, and pointing out certain instances of work deficiencies. The essence had to remain untouchable: a daily succession of victories in the building of socialism, the center of the international scene being occupied by Cuba and the world's most influential leader being Fidel Castro. Another anniversary was being celebrated around that time, the death of Tania, the guerrilla who had fought in the mountains of Bolivia with Che Guevara. One of *Granma*'s six pages was filled with this subject. I suggested to Carlos Rafael that if he looked through *Granma*'s files, he'd see that each year for the last twenty years the same article had been repeated. "Yes," he said with a smile, "maybe a page that says nothing new is a lot of space these days." A proposal had also been made that the ministries have official spokesmen so that journalists could report on the news faster. This would have meant adding one more link to the chain of waiting, for a spokesman would have to consult with a minister, the minister with the State Council, the Council functionary with . . . They would doubtless wind up publishing an official speech on Angola or on the construction of new highways in the allotted space.

Lázaro Barredo's dialogue with the leftist weekly *El Periodista*—which stopped publishing due to the Argentine economic crisis—has some telling lines.

Question: Can we conceive the hypothesis whereby, as occurs in any capitalist country, an editorial in a Cuban newspaper will be able to criticize some decision made by the head of the government?

Answer: That's a bit complicated. We're in a position to make an extraordinary effort but not about to engage in liberalism. We will not go to that extreme.

How far they are prepared to go was the focus of the exchange of ideas on journalism that I had with Vice-President Rodríguez. I think he began to doubt the need of the editor in chief to travel abroad. He confessed that the solution might be in the quality and range of the news, in the scope of the coverage, and not in the hierarchical structure whereby those with revolutionary merits are placed on top. I thought Rodríguez was ready for a proposal that occurred to me just then: to allow three foreign journalists, with a small crew, to prepare every day for a month an alternative edition of *Granma,* of which a small number of copies would be printed. Every morning, Fidel Castro and a few government members could compare the official *Granma* with the private *Granma.*

Carlos Rafael is a man with a warm, ready laugh. The idea amused him. The three professionals, I added, could be Rogelio García Lupo, one of the founders of the official news agency Prensa Latina in the early days of the Revolution, an Argentine living in Buenos Aires; Isidoro Gilbert, from the Soviet news agency Tass, who also lives in Buenos Aires; and myself, born in the Ukraine, with dual Argentine and Israeli nationality. I sketched an outline of how we would work.

"We have problems, but not to that extent," was his reply. "That far we won't go."

Two years after that conversation, in July 1989, the journalist Alfonso Muñoz Unsain, an Argentine who has worked for Agence France Presse in Havana for a couple of decades, sent an article to the Buenos Aires newspaper *Nuevo Sur,* in which he said: "The relationship in Cuba between reality and the press generally borders on the schizophrenic." Recalling Carlos Rafael Rodríguez's statement, one would have to add that Castroism prefers to remain with its problems, and with schizophrenia, rather than grant Cubans the freedom to gaze at reality.

As the evening with the journalists seemed to be concluding, I added yet another element to the naked diagnosis I'd made of the Cuban press, as if to break the ice. Maybe, I told them, they should import Jewish journalists. Jews have brought to our profession two elements—part of Jewish culture—without which journalism can't function: irony and skepticism. Might not this be the antidote to the spirit of complacency and intellectual subjugation characteristic of the profession on the island?

But we were Latin American journalists—which meant

that the evening couldn't truly come to an end without talk about women. No one in Cuba, of course, would have thought to invite a female colleague. The sexes were more differentiated than may be assumed from the declamations of women holding high positions.

There was nothing salacious. Eros is amply gratified in Cuba and needs no stimulation. Among men, talking about women, especially mulatto women, is more a cultural rite than macho crudity. Naturally one had to be careful not to commit any political transgressions, and even more, to avoid their becoming public.

This subject had already led to the expulsion of a foreign correspondent—the result, specifically, of a dispatch on the clandestine export of mulatto women to obtain Western currency through alleged matrimonial agencies. In 1985, Andrei Biroukof, of Agence France Presse, sent an article to Paris on what he viewed as a virtual slave trade. This occurred at the time of the meeting of the World Congress of Women in New Delhi. The Cuban delegate, Vilma Espin, the wife of Raúl Castro, ordered Biroukof's expulsion.

This incident led me to suspect, on reading the news accounts in June 1989 about the drug trafficking carried on by General Arnaldo Ochoa and high government officials, that it, too, might have been organized to obtain dollars, with which to import Western goods. Muñoz Unsain, the veteran Havana journalist, ventured a figure of four billion dollars that Cuba hoped to make from the Medellín drug cartel.

Naturally, in private conversation, there are numerous references to mulatto women who are available to special guests in protocol houses. But you don't have to listen to rumors. All you need do is look around the streets, restaurants, hotels, beaches, museums, and movie houses.

In 1966, when Fidel Castro had to dispose of certain

high officials suspected of disloyalty, he organized the so-called "Dolce Vita Trial." On this occasion, at least, the regime wasn't obliged to fabricate evidence, for it was within arm's reach and public knowledge. The most prominent offender was Comandante Efigenio Ameijeiras, chief of the National Police, who was accused of leading a dissolute life. Twenty-three years later, on June 13, 1989, the official newspaper *Granma* announced that Diocles Torralbas, minister of transportation and one of the vice-presidents of the Council of Ministers, had been dismissed from his posts on charges of corruption and dissolute behavior. He had been one of the guerrilla chiefs in the battle against corruption during the Batista period, but no one in Havana was unaware of his taste for luxury and pretty girls. His downfall was not in fact due to that, though it was the formula chosen to penalize him for his friendship with Arnaldo Ochoa. After the dismissal proceedings, there was similarly no need for the courts to drum up evidence to sentence him to twenty years in jail.

The female backside in general, and that of the mulatto woman in particular, occupies a prominent position in daily life. Women display their backsides—the bigger the better—wag them freely and rhythmically, and welcome appreciative gazes with a smile. I happened to be seated at a table near the Floridita dining room, pensively beholding the enormous backside of a woman seated on one of the high stools facing the bar where Hemingway had also drunk. The woman was wearing very, but very, tight red pants. She was young, and her prominent rump had not a single excess ounce of fat. The man accompanying her looked at me, placed his hand on her backside, stroked it, and smiled.

Yes, people tell me, it's the Caribbean, the heat, Africa, music, the smell of vegetation, slavery, the mixture of cultures. The Revolution granted universal rights regardless of sex, but no revolution could be more potent than Cuban eroticism or Soviet alcoholism. The sexes had been equalized in Cuba, but backsides had particular values and meanings, a distinction much more significant here than in other cultures.

According to the versions of people familiar with the Andrei Biroukof investigations, a mulatto woman married by proxy to someone abroad through the Cuban matrimonial agency, and authorized to leave the island to unite with her spouse, could mean an infusion of up to $14,000 for the depleted vaults of the national treasury.

In order to convey values more clearly to me, someone explains that one of the most important Cuban paintings of the thirties is devoted precisely to mulatto backsides. In 1925, a group of painters—Victor Manuel García, Fidelio Ponce de León, Eduardo Abela, Carlos Enríquez, Marcelo Pogolotti, Antonio Gattorno—rebelled against the ruling academism and, influenced by avant-garde aesthetics emanating from Europe, set out to create their own vision of Cuban reality. Their paintings are now grouped on the second floor, galleries IX and X, of the National Museum in the Palace of Fine Arts. (A decade is still needed for the great talents of Rene Portocarrero and Wilfredo Lam to emerge.)

The most impressive work, occupying a privileged position in the Palace of Fine Arts, is *El Rapto de las Mulatas* (The Kidnapping of the Mulattos), painted in 1938 by Carlos Enríquez. The entire painting, 5½ by 3¾ feet in size, is permeated with mulatto color. Two horsemen flaunting bandoliers—latifundia overseers, highway robbers, or guerrillas—are carrying off two mulatto women amid a confused mass of rounded forms composed of women's backsides and horses' rumps. The harmonious fusion of those carnal spheres is striking, with its merged, intertwined curves, an explosion of temptations and stimuli in one splendid ode of joy.

There is, throughout the island, a perpetual manifestation of fresh, ingenuous eroticism that transcends the promotional artifices which take the joy out of sex in more advanced societies. Thus I wasn't surprised when people urged that I look at the canvas painted by Carlos Enríquez, who died in 1956, before the Revolution.

The regime, which thinks that it is combating this Cuban sexuality, regarded it as an achievement when Jesús Díaz, the writer who best expresses the party line, published a book, excellently written, whose theme is a Communist's trial by his own cell. Judged not for an isolated deed but for his entire being, he is forced to recount his whole life. Such sessions, commonplace in Cuba, can last several days. The book was attempting, I think, to demystify somewhat this peculiar mechanism, which gives rise to instances of personal vindictiveness and political intrigues.

In reply to the questions of the tribunal, aimed at determining whether he can remain a Party member, the subject confesses that his wife had a lover and that he forgave her. The novelist presents this pardon sympathetically, and, coming from a writer who belongs to the regime, this can be interpreted as a guiding code, a message on the correct position to be adopted by a true revolutionary.

I made no attempt at even discussing the outrage and humiliation involved in the procedure, or the violation of an individual's rights to privacy. Debating this aspect would, once again, plunge me totally into the realm of ideology, the struggle against imperialism, would remind me yet again of the plaque cemented on a wall at the corner of Twelfth Street and Twenty-third Avenue in Havana: "What the imperialists can't forgive us for is having forged a socialist revolution under the very nose of the United States." At which point one would have to debate whether it was socialist or simply totalitarian.

But I did try to discuss the subject of the pardon. What to the author and other commentators seemed like an invitation to redemption suggested to me a more complex constellation of consequences. In sexually permissive Cuban society, totally unmodified by the Revolution, the debate in the Communist cell regarding the couple's private life, and the pardon granted by the man, was an exercise in hypocrisy—yet one more such. But it was also a way of sustaining the macho role within the Cuban reality and of indicating to women the limits of their position. Yes, a woman could excel in her sexual function, but she was forbidden to make the decision in the erotic relationship. The more her freedom was curtailed, the greater intensity—that is, voluptuousness—she would presumably express in the limited area assigned her.

This is just one of the aspects of the intricate web within which life proceeds for this high-spirited people confined in an authoritarian world. Whether in the message novel, tropical romanticism, party proclamations, or televised messages from El Comandante, the only thing that has been modified is the language of the explanations—or the explanations themselves—of Cuban attitudes. The New Man, as defined and described by Che Guevara and Fidel Castro, who proclaimed his birth or imminent birth, has not emerged, but clearly Cubans themselves have no notion of what he's all about, nor do they believe in his existence, or even that he will ever appear. It is the persistent, all-pervasive, joyous eroticism that attracts so much tourism, a factor that the regime is reluctant to admit.

Enumerating the jokes that relate to eroticism and the interpretation of the multiple codes would produce an

endless list, a substantial document of collective waggish-
ness. In this area, Cubans are not particularly concerned
about protocol. The official explanation for justifying El
Comandante's various domiciles—security—is acceptable in view of the CIA's numerous attempts to assassinate him. Cuban street wisdom, ironical and slanderous
as under every totalitarian regime, has it that this is the
only possible way for Fidel to attend to all his lovers.
When I asked a young woman if Fidel had many children as a result of this way of life, she replied, "Of
course. What Cuban woman would take the pill when
going to bed with Fidel?"

Quite a number of tourists are coming to Cuba because the trip and the two-week stay are subsidized by
the government and because they dream about the hot
island. At breakfast, I happened to share a table in the
hotel dining room with two Spaniards who had arrived
that very morning. I assumed that they felt committed
to the Revolution—they looked to be in their thirties—
but no, not at all. They were unenthusiastic about the
countrywide tour that had been laid out for them. They
would have preferred to remain in Havana.

Elections had taken place in Spain recently, but the
Spaniard from Oviedo hadn't voted because politics didn't
interest him. The man from Barcelona—who indicated
that he was born in Valencia—had cast his vote for the
center right. They had come to Cuba for the mulatto
women.

After this confession, they began questioning me. My
first answer was that the increase in AIDS was due to the
soldiers returning from Angola and Ethiopia, epidemic
areas. The man from Oviedo had brought a dozen con-
doms for his two-week stay; the one from Barcelona two
dozen.

The topic most important to them was the question of

where. I explained hotel rules. The women who run the elevators don't allow anyone to even enter the cabs without showing guest identification. I assumed that the operators were under police control.

A few hours later, after lunch, the men told me that there were lots of girls at the hotel swimming pool in the daytime and in nearby streets at night. They're called *jinetas,* or jockeys, for obvious reasons. They're also called *cubanas fleteras,* taxi-girls. Two hotel attendants monitor entry into the rooms. The Spaniards already had everything set for that night; they were leaving the following morning with a group of tourists for the interior of the island, in accordance with the scheduled itinerary. They were not at all pleased with the idea of leaving Havana.

I later established that they hadn't lied about the access system to the rooms and about poolside propositions. The Revolution could do nothing to steer or rechannel the energy which Cubans assign to eroticism. Whenever an attempt was made to impose discipline or disseminate moral prescriptions, it failed. The one substantial modification produced by the Revolution in relations between the sexes was an incredible increase in the number of divorces.

In a country without statistics, or with statistics placed at the service of a political goal, the only means of gaining an approximate notion of the marital situation is to raise the subject in conversation. What emerged from such dialogues, where a casual tone replaced the questions of a poll, was a revealing panorama of family life, relationships between couples, divorce as the most direct escape from grueling problems.

The grueling problems that provoked an explosive outbreak of divorce in the last fifteen years have stemmed more than anything else from the terrible housing shortage.

After the Revolution, construction began on the typical housing projects found in all modern cities, two- or three-bedroom units. But since the initial drive, fewer and fewer have been built. These buildings are seriously impaired by the low quality of materials used, errors in design, shortages of water and electricity. When a window is broken, it's very hard to replace it, owing to an acute shortage of glass. It is even more serious when a pipe breaks, for it takes weeks to get permission for a replacement. There is no paint, and almost all the dwellings I visited still have their original coat. Serious errors in design have been committed despite the time and money invested in conceiving an architecture to serve the Caribbean and the Revolution.

Here is where one senses most the disaster incurred by intolerance toward experts who failed to adapt, because they either would not or could not, to the state of permanent intrigue of the Castro Revolution. If you weren't good at dealing with the bureaucratic machinations, if you didn't proclaim the Revolution to be more efficient than the simple efficiency of your trade, you were most unlikely to be called upon to participate in construction plans. An architect told me he had sought refuge in the university, giving a course in the history of architecture, since there was no longer anything to construct, nor did it make sense anymore to teach design in a country where an architect's only opportunities are stymied by bureaucracy and its stifling planning terminology.

Fidel Castro, in his own verbose, repetitive, and generally incoherent way, presented the same view in his 1986 speech at the Joint Session of the Central Committee of the Communist Party of Cuba. As quoted in the September–October issue of the magazine *Cuba Socialista*, El Comandante said: "We have taught much Marxism, and provided many people with dialectical materialism, historical materialism, tons of things. Never, I believe, have books, articles, writings, talks, or lectures on Marxism been wanting, but we haven't taught the people that a citizen's number one duty is to work and produce seriously, responsibly, and with discipline. Reading about the things going on all over, one must draw the conclusion that the notions of responsibility, duty, and work have been lost here. This, I sincerely believe, is our number one problem, the disease we must fight."

Prerevolutionary housing is in an indescribable state of deterioration. And the wooden shacks in the outlying quarters continue to serve the same function as in the times of Batista.

Dwellings have been divided and subdivided. Mattresses are scattered on the floors, in courtyards and corridors, and are aired during the day. They're placed according to a prearranged pattern, allowing an open path that everyone knows. It would be dangerous otherwise, for someone coming home late or wanting to use the toilet during the night could step on the head of a neighbor or a family member.

The rooms are divided by sheets hung wall to wall on ropes. If someone has political access to the officials who allot material, it's possible to obtain bricks, plasterboard, glass, wood, perhaps a little zinc, with which the subdivisions are improved. The hardest articles to obtain are still paint and glass.

In such places there is constant flux among the population, owing to marriage, birth, moves. And everything must be fitted into the existing structure. The heat, the lack of water and light, long lines in front of toilets early in the morning, are the other elements that have led to the erosion of the nuclear family and the proliferation of divorces.

When you walk through Havana, it's painful to see those

marvelous Spanish colonial houses that, though bursting with inhabitants, seem deserted and abandoned. You feel the loss of that "city of columns," as Alejo Carpentier called it: "Havana colonnades, flanking their marble Carlos II, their emblematic lions, their Indian ruling over a fountain of Greek dolphins—evoking potential jungle trunks, shafts of rostral columns, inconceivable forums—making me think of Baudelaire's lines referring to the *'temple où de vivants piliers / laissaient entendre de confuses paroles.'* "

The Revolution wouldn't have had to divert funds from any priority in order to preserve the beauty of that little columned Havana. But sad as is the aesthetic loss, one senses that something more profound has occurred: the perversion of family ethics. The loss of family identity was evolving at the same time that seminars of architects invited to Cuba were waxing enthusiastic over the possibility of a revolutionary aesthetic in housing theory and a revolutionary ethic in the workers' attitude during the construction of that housing.

A large proportion of Cubans live together: couples with a set of parents or grandparents, or with aunts and uncles unable to fend for themselves, or a home subdivided among the nuclear family. Quarrels, accusations, shouting, are replacing family solidarity.

The regime's reaction, once again, was long-winded and pathetic. Government-run love hotels began to multiply. The problems of the nuclear family weren't resolved, but at least the hotels allowed a married couple to have an intimate hour together, without the humiliation of having to stifle sighs and outcries behind a sheet or a screen in their own home.

Like many of these couples, I stood in line to enter El Aseo (The Cleaning Place), a love hotel in Old Havana, next to the railway station.

One evening as I was leaving the Floridita, a girl was waiting on Bélgica Avenue, to the left. Another prostitute was next to the statue of Francisco de Albear, to the right, on Obispo Street. For some reason, the girl standing in the little square struck me as more typically Cuban, against the background of the stone figure of someone who in the late nineteenth century organized the drainage systems of Havana.

Prostitutes in Havana are as important a source of information as are taxi drivers in democratic societies. I don't understand why Castroism insists that the Revolution has eliminated prostitution through a reeducation campaign. It's a profession that has endured, with only small modifications to adapt to the times. The explanation for its survival lies more in the field of anthropology than in sociology or economics.

In Cuba you encounter prostitutes everywhere. Those flocking to the hotels are for the most part college graduates or dropouts. I assumed that this was due to their knowledge of English, but I was informed that it stemmed from their having a greater craving for consumer goods than did working-class women, and that these commodities were available only in stores catering to tourists and high state functionaries. It may be more complicated than that, but possibly this craving is whetted by access to information on fashions and products; or by belonging to what was once the middle class and retaining the manners and culture to move comfortably among foreigners.

The women prefer not to ask for money, for dollar stores require identity papers to validate purchases, whereas in stores for Cubans, only national currency can be used, and the shelves are empty. If the women collect in foreign currency, they can go to the black market, with its risks. They prefer an invitation to spend a few days in Varadero, or at the Hemingway Marina or any other beach spot, or to enjoy one long day at a big hotel, getting some products from the tourist shops. They stock up on lipstick, mascara, chocolate, underwear, stockings, jeans, artificial pearl necklaces, earrings, shoes, blouses, bathing suits. At poolside, they eat lobster and sip rum.

The humblest women, those on the street, generally unemployed, accept Cuban pesos. They are afraid to go into big hotels because their impoverished appearance betrays them, and the elevator operators don't allow them to go up to the rooms.

The girl in the square agrees to tell me what happens when she finds a client and to show me how she operates, where she takes the man, the streets she covers, and how she avoids the police. She's very poor, wants only Cuban pesos because she's unemployed, and anyhow wouldn't know what to do with dollars. I hand her the Cuban money I have on me. And so we come to El Aseo. Patiently we wait our turn on line in the street, and finally we enter the waiting room. Everything is very dirty and, like every-where else, poorly lit. The heat is infernal, people speak in whispers, some women are sewing. The girl waits for the best room to be free, the one that has a small fan that works. She tells me that there's not a single prostitute in the waiting room, that most clients appear to be married cou-ples. The room we are taken to has a naked electric bulb hanging from the ceiling, a dirty sheet, an empty bucket on the floor and another one with water, plus a towel. Music is blaring from a loudspeaker, and the fan works.

This filthy, squalid place is, for many, a resource for preserving a married couple's intimacy. The attendant asks for payment in advance, but doesn't accept dollars, since the place isn't for tourists. He dare not ignore the rule; punishment can be very severe. I tell him I only want to stay for ten minutes to chat with the girl, which scares him even more, and he practically throws us out. He's so nervous that he thinks my Spanish is Italian, and that's what he speaks to me.

When we leave, the girl and I walk toward the nearby square—a hangout, she tells me, for buying black market dollars. But it's late, and the square is almost deserted. The night is warm, the sky blue, the perfume of vegetation is a garment covering one's body. I could have lingered here for hours, but the girl insisted on telling me her life story, all her misery. It became unbearable.

In a discussion I had with the novelist Jesús Díaz, he dwelt on schemes hatched by the New York and Miami Mafia: plots by George Raft, Meyer Lansky, and Albert Anastasia to fill the 150 kilometers of coastline extending from Havana to Varadero with hotels, gambling casinos, brothels, and drug houses. In the course of my trip, I didn't encounter any casinos. As for drugs, they circulate on levels I heard about but didn't investigate. I sense, however, that the regime's urgency to acquire dollars will soon prompt it to create tourist zones where everything will be allowed, no questions asked. In such an atmosphere, Cubans in Miami will be able to send family members the commodities unavailable in Cuba.

As I'm leaving Varadero for Havana one day, a young man signals to me. I take him to the city of Matanzas, about forty kilometers away. He's a schoolteacher and has been waiting two years for an allotment of bricks to partition a room in his mother's house. Then he can get married. Meanwhile, the hotels. There's no necessity to use the poorest and dirtiest in Havana, as I did with El Aseo. People with their own car or an official one, the perquisite of a bureaucratic position, or those who can afford a taxi, choose one of the facilities on the outskirts of Havana, which have gardens, air-conditioning, hot and cold running water, optional music in the rooms, a bar, and a congenial atmosphere.

When we reached Matanzas, he pointed to a tall apartment building under construction. How did they get the materials? I ask. The building belongs to the Construction Workers Union and is reserved for its members, he answers.

Before entering Havana, coming from Matanzas, you pass through Cojímar, the small fishing port that has been converted into a permanent monument to Ernest Hemingway, who used to go out fishing from there. There the fishing contest is held in his honor; and there, in May 1960, a year and a half after the triumph of the Revolution, Ernest Hemingway and Fidel Castro met for the first time, on the occasion of the first fishing contest. Numerous photographs of that meeting exist, but no records of anything noteworthy spoken before the scores of witnesses— only a few formalities.

The revolutionaries never viewed Hemingway sympathetically. He had taken little interest in Cuba (where he had a house for two decades), or in the fight against Batista, or in the bearded guerrillas of the Sierra Maestra. The Hemingway cult as embodied in the museum established at his home, Finca Vigía, in the municipality of San Francisco de Paula, a southeastern suburb of Havana, is aimed more at tourism and propaganda than anything else.

It is undoubtedly a successful operation, for I had the impression that no other place in Cuba is visited by more tourists than Finca Vigía, nor with as much pleasure.

In July 1961, one year after the meeting with Castro, Hemingway committed suicide in his home in the United States, so as not to face the deterioration of his ailing body. Organization of the museum began that same year. But the regime has never managed to establish a solid link between Hemingway and Castroism. Attempts have been made ever since his death, and continue still, to prove ympathy on the writer's part—affinities, a declaration, a gesture. The tourist gets the impression that Hemingway supported the Revolution and Fidel Castro, that the writer is part of the Cuban Revolution. Nowhere is it stated explicitly, as if to rectify a mistaken notion, but it's insinuated time and again.

The cult is geared toward perpetuating the myth, toward creating a sense that Hemingway belonged, toward convincing people that Hemingway is the North American of the Revolution.

The prologue written by García Márquez for Norberto Fuentes's *Hemingway in Cuba*, published in 1986, reflects what Castroists hope will be tourists' conception of the writer. The Cuban journalist's book records excessive details of the writer's life on the island. García Márquez entitles his prologue "Our Hemingway," but he never ventures to explain the "our." Hemingway is too famous for such a distortion to go unremarked. García Márquez writes: "Another highly controversial aspect of Hemingway in his last years was his position toward the Cuban Revolution. Though there's no recorded opinion of public approval, there isn't, to anyone's knowledge, any of disagreement, other than some rather untrustworthy statements attributed to him by biased biographers as having been stated privately."

The remark is exquisite sophistry. To regard a subject as controversial because of the absence of an expressed preference—that is, a nonexpression—is a peculiar assessment. Wouldn't it be easier to say that if Hemingway never expressed himself on the subject it was because he wasn't interested?

This disinterest of his was common knowledge in Cuba and may have been one of the reasons an honest writer, Edmundo Desnoes, criticized him in an essay published in 1967. Another writer, Lisandro Otero, linked to the regime, gave his own version, one totally impossible to con-firm. In a 1963 article on Hemingway, he included a com-ment that propaganda eventually transformed into truth. According to Otero, Hemingway once said: "Had I been a few years younger, I would have climbed the Sierra Maestra with Fidel Castro."

No one doubts this to be a fabrication. Just as no one doubts that the statement made by his widow, Mary, to the journalist Luis Báez, and published in *Bohemia* maga-zine in 1977, was part of a deal: "Hemingway was always in favor of the Revolution." If this statement is true, how curious that Hemingway never made his feelings known. It's also possible, of course, that the writer's widow was trying to recover some of the items left at Finca Vigía.

An Argentine journalist, Rodolfo Walsh, who was living in Havana as organizer of Prensa Latina, almost managed to draw a statement from Ernest Hemingway himself. But the reply had little relation to the journalist's incisive, pointed questions amid the tumult of the Havana airport in 1960, on the writer's final departure from the island. There were nine words in Spanish, though Walsh had questioned him in English: *"Vamos a ganar. Nosotros los cubanos vamos a ganar."* (We are going to win. We Cu-bans are going to win.) And then he added on his own, this time in English: "I'm not a Yankee, you know."

Ever since, people have made what they will of these words, the writer's only specific reference to a country that for years had been undergoing a cruel revolutionary struggle and for seventeen months had been ruled by a leader who occupied page one of the newspaper, but whom Hemingway never publicly mentioned.

Walsh's so-called report was presented as a journalistic triumph. He returned to Argentina to join the leftist guer-rillas, and in the seventies led a terrorist shock group which became a kind of executive arm. Before the military dictatorship, the group had organized and led the attack on the metallurgical union to assassinate its leader, Augusto Vandor, who had displayed too much independence from Juan Domingo Perón, exiled in Madrid. The leftist guerrillas wished to demonstrate their Peronist loyalties.

Walsh also acted in numerous terrorist operations against the military dictatorship that began in Argentina in 1976, and one year later, in March 1977, he was kidnapped by the military and joined the ranks of the thousands who disappeared.

With the exception of Fidel Castro and Che Guevara, no worship is promoted more in Cuba than that of Ernest Hemingway. The day of my visit to the museum at Finca Vigía, I find a group of Italians, Bulgarians, and two young socialist women from West Germany, Ana and Susana, with whom I have lunch at Cojímar before returning to Havana. Neither of them knows Spanish, but one speaks rudimentary English. Their coming to Cuba was impelled by two combined powerful forces: Che Guevara's image and the low cost of visits as organized by the Cuban tourist agency.

I have made the ritual tour recommended in the Finca Vigía guidebook. Everything is familiar from my readings, and everything is moving. Naturally there's a photograph of Spencer Tracy during the filming of *The Old Man and the Sea* in 1955. Hemingway's love of fishing, hunting, bulls, his whims and friendships, are evident throughout the house and in the gardens. At the base of the adjacent tower there are, in addition to the first edition of *Death in the Afternoon,* 1932, two bullfighting caps and twenty-eight photographs of bullfighting scenes. One of the photos shows Ignacio Sánchez Mejías in one of his passes, and beneath it Hemingway's opinion: "Though I respect his bravery, his skill with the darts and his insolence, I don't care for him as a bullfighter, as a banderillero, or as a man."

I pause in front of this photograph because it was this bullfighter's death that stirred the poet García Lorca to write his long "Lament for Ignacio Sánchez Mejías," depicting a thoroughly different matador: *"No hubo príncipe en Sevilla / que comparársele pueda, / ni espada como su espada / ni corazón tan de veras"* (No prince in Seville / can compare with him, / no sword like his sword / nor heart so true). *"Tardará mucho tiempo en nacer, si es que nace, / un andaluz tan claro, tan rico de aventura"* (A long time will pass before another such as he is born, if ever another is, / an Andalusian so illustrious, so rich in adventure).

I wander through the environs of Finca Vigía, which you enter by crossing a modest street with small wooden houses, where Hemingway's original neighbors still live. When you talk to them, their comments express the official cult rather than nostalgia—a cult so well organized that it prompted García Márquez's 1982 statement in reference to Fidel Castro: "In his long, frequent trips to the interior of the country, he always carries in his car a jumbled pile of government documents to study, and you often see among them two red-covered volumes of Hemingway's selected works." Hard to believe, despite the pleasure El Comandante may take from reading them.

In one of the houses on that street, in the open veranda at the top of three steps, an old woman is seated. She lets me rest a bit after I've asked for a glass of water. A slight, gray-haired woman. Seated on a rocking chair, I keep her company, as she waits for the milkman, who's late this August Sunday. Josefina Anía, seventy-nine years old, has lived here for half a century. Her children played with Hemingway's, but she didn't find the writer a likable neighbor. His widow, on the other hand, was a pleasant person. Her arrival was expected, and it would have been nice to chat with her; but she didn't come. Doña Josefina's two daughters live in Cuba and look after her. Her three sons went to Miami.

No one can truly know what Hemingway thought of Fidel Castro and his revolution. The cult devoted to the writer, as contrived by the regime, is hypocritical from the political point of view, and certainly wouldn't exist were it not so effective in promoting tourism. But to say "Our Hemingway" is taking propaganda too far.

I return to Havana.

Along the highway are the recurrent posters I've seen elsewhere in Cuba. A mixture of philosophy, promise, threat, and instruction: "Discipline. Efficiency. Production"; "Here you work for an ideal, not for money."

There's no commercial advertising, of course. I wonder whether it wouldn't be preferable to be subjected to subliminal pressures so as to be a consumer of a particular toothpaste rather than be forcibly plunged into the collective misery described as a happy, victorious society.

In Havana, good news awaits me. A European journalist, accredited in Cuba, has agreed to put me in contact with Elizardo Sánchez, president of the Cuban Commission of Human Rights and National Reconciliation. My friend knows the risks he's taking. A year before, in September 1986, the head of the Reuters office and a journalist from Agence France Presse were expelled from the country for having interviewed Sánchez. The journalist takes me to the vicinity of Elizardo Sánchez's home, indicates how to get to it on foot, and hurries away. The old drama of accredited foreign correspondents in totalitarian countries, ever threatened by expulsion, was something never well received by their bosses.

News organizations prefer less news and greater administrative stability.

Since that meeting at Elizardo's home, I've read various statements he's made, articles in different media on the history of his sacrifices and imprisonments, reports of human rights organizations, details revealed at meetings for freedom of expression.

Recently I saw his face in *Newsweek* magazine illustrating an interview with the journalist Stryker McGuire, and also in a dialogue on television's CNN channel. On my desk I have the photographs I took at his house.

When I visit him, on August 28, 1987, his wife has just phoned from Miami. I react by doing what one stupidly does in such instances: I try to console him by recalling the time that I myself was imprisoned, not knowing if my wife and children were alive or had been "disappeared" by the military.

It's easier to offer consolation than to enter Elizardo's world. But he isn't looking for consolation. He has been imprisoned several times since 1972. For years he's been trying to reclaim his professorship of philosophy at the University of Havana, from which he was expelled for having defended a version of Marxism that differed from the official one. There used to be fourteen people in the paternal home, and nine have already emigrated. I have lunch with the remaining household members, including the old father and a family of Jehovah's Witnesses who have sought asylum. Fidel Castro is obsessively antagonistic to this religious group, as were the military in Argentina.

So here is Elizardo Sánchez, victim of a Communist dictatorship, recounting events such as I myself suffered as a victim of a Fascist dictatorship.

He is drawn to hidden meanings, understandably so for someone trying to discern them in the cruel, despairing world of Castroism. He seats me in the same chair that was once occupied by the New York lawyer Steve Kass, a human rights activist. He regards this coincidence as one more piece of evidence that prospects are improving, that the future is promising.

Elizardo senses that the details he provides on the violence suffered by prisoners in Cuban jails create great anxiety in me. Fortunately, his combative equipment extends beyond a catalogue of accusations.

His house was repeatedly broken into by the police, in search of documents and subversive programs. But what can they find, he says with a smile, when our program is simply the Declaration of the United Nations on the Rights of Man, which Cuba has accepted? During the hours I spend at his house, the door leading to the street remains open. Elizardo wants to demonstrate that you can live in Castro's Cuba without being afraid.

Elizardo's father presides at the table during lunch and receives all the honors of a traditional Hispanic family. Almost completely deaf, he observes us with lively eyes and tries to understand. He's a retired railroad worker, just like García Márquez's father, says Elizardo.

Elizardo gets around the city on a bicycle, one of those ancient, dilapidated vehicles you see on Israeli kibbutzim, and he accompanied me on it to the avenue, where I waited for an hour until a taxi passed. Luckily, the driver recognized that I was a tourist and would pay in dollars. A writer seated on the bar of a bicycle being pedaled up to the hotel by someone persecuted by the regime would have been absurd.

A few days later, a group of human rights activists ask, through a friend, to see me. I invite them to the hotel terrace, in full view, to protect them at least a bit by showing that they're not engaging in clandestine activity, and also to confirm the regime's strategy toward such meetings. The head of the group is Ricardo Bofill, president of the Cuban Committee for Human Rights. I notice that we're being filmed from the rooftop of a school across the street, but at this point I don't think it matters very much. The regime is weakening day by day.

Bofill insists that the government must recognize the legal existence of this committee, but most of those present, all prison veterans, are hoping for permission to leave the country. Some finally obtained it, including Bofill.

But such is not the case with Sánchez.

He doesn't think it possible for a Cuban to separate the struggle for human rights from the quest for a political solution. It is precisely because his group is looking for a political solution that it's called the Cuban Commission of Human Rights and National Reconciliation. "Reconciliation" encompasses all the violence unleashed upon Cuba since the start of the century, in the wake of independence, with nothing excluded. He thinks that exclusions can lead only to civil war.

Like Martin Luther King, Jr., Elizardo has a dream. He has explained it to everyone who has interviewed him, has mailed it to a list extending from Nancy Reagan to Queen Sofia of Spain. I suggest to him that Danielle Mitterrand will understand it better than Nancy Reagan.

The dream has an implacable logic. When he explained it to me, he emphasized that one of his inspirations was the Pole Jacek Kuron, from Solidarity. In view of the course of events in Poland subsequent to our interview, and the political transformations in the Soviet Union and in Hungary, Elizardo's dream ought not to strike us as absurd.

Yet it is. I can't picture Fidel Castro tolerating a Lech Walesa, who in Cuba would be condemned to twenty years' imprisonment even before delivering his first speech. Nor do I believe that El Comandante is capable of becoming a Gorbachev.

But Elizardo insists that Cuban society must be changed. The dilemma is not socialism or capitalism but the modification of a community that for thirty years has been unable to develop a way of life other than hatred and fear, or a system other than violence.

Whether Elizardo Sánchez believes in the possibility of Fidel Castro accepting a modification of his dictatorial exercise of power, I couldn't say. When I ask him this, he doesn't comment specifically on El Comandante but evaluates the situation as a whole: If there's no gradual, peaceful reform of the system under Fidel Castro himself, the only alternative will be a coup against Castro.

In August 1987, Elizardo thought that if there were even a suspicion of such a coup afoot, the brothers Raúl and Fidel Castro would impose a bloody repression. The events of July 1989—the shooting of General Ochoa and his collaborators, the high-level purges—would tend to confirm Elizardo's thesis, for it's very possible that the drug-trafficking accusation was a cover-up to conceal a planned coup d'état. Pure, simple logic compels the conclusion that it's impossible, in a dictatorship where mutual spying among the leaders is the foundation of its permanence, to have vast, complex operations of drug shipments and capital transactions occurring without the Castro brothers' knowledge. A capital negotiation, controlled by a government firm, would be directly responsible, without intermediaries, to Fidel Castro.

Elizardo feels that there can be a change within the system. If one looks toward Eastern Europe, I suppose, one can theoretically believe that a humanist can also be a Communist. In those countries where candidates face each other in free elections, representatives of the Communist

Party come off poorly. But Elizardo doesn't even care to speculate on the possibility of abandoning the present system. Actually, he fears a civil war. Here the humanist overrides the Communist who coined the fervent statement about violence opening the doors of history.

Sánchez rejects the leftist communism of Castro and proposes a transition based on reforms that don't destroy the system but mobilize it in the direction of social democracy. That is the goal of his Commission of Human Rights. Once human rights are restored, the next step would be an agreement between both Cuban communities, the one on the island and the one in Miami. That is the goal of his Commission of National Reconciliation.

If all these elements were put into a computer, the answer would be similar to Elizardo's dream. After all, Cuba lives off Soviet subsidies, and El Comandante could not survive serious pressure from Mikhail Gorbachev. Accommodation between the United States and the Soviet Union is a process involving more important subjects than Cuba, such as disarmament. Hence, Elizardo believes, the United States could engage in blocking the activity of extreme rightist groups in Miami, by encouraging a democratic leadership in the exile community and allowing Cubans to invest the necessary capital for rebuilding the island.

Since our interview in 1987, during which both of us were somewhat hopeful about democratic Latin American governments, Elizardo has moved increasingly in this direction. It seemed, when we met in Havana, that the group of eight countries composed of Argentina, Panama, Brazil, Peru, Venezuela, Colombia, Uruguay, and Mexico was in a position to obtain a certain liberalization from both Havana and Washington. But the two capitals stuck to their all-or-nothing position. At this point, the economic deterioration in these eight democracies has barely allowed them enough energy to beg for credit in financial centers.

For Elizardo, what remains are Moscow and Washington, a bicycle, a shirt, a pair of trousers, a pair of shoes, and the open door of his house, proof that one need not be intimidated by the dictatorship.

There's something enviable in someone's ability to build the patent optimism that I observed in Elizardo on such meager, absurd elements, within a society he himself described for *Newsweek* in July 1989 in the following terms: "Our society is so sick with hatred that any attempt to overthrow the current system would have a terrible effect. Blood would run in the streets."

He is seeking help for his project and reads me the names of Argentines on the Cuban Commission of Human Rights. He also reads a declaration of support sent him from Buenos Aires. It's painful to have to discourage him. All the signatories, led by a right-wing politician, Alvaro Alsogaray, were accomplices of the genocidal Fascist military dictatorship that existed in Argentina between 1976 and 1983, and even now are friends of CIA-backed terrorists in Miami.

Elizardo, who didn't know those individuals, remarks that from such a distance and with scant communication, it's hard to choose one's allies. He mentions that owing to situations like this, which are beyond its control, his group is accused of being CIA marionettes, something especially painful to him, for he regards himself as a socialist. In the years he has spent fighting for human rights, being manipulated has been as great a danger as being thrown into prison.

Those who can be manipulated by the CIA or by the Cuban secret service are Americans falsely accused, as it later turns out, and Cubans infiltrated into human rights organizations who publicly acknowledge having received money and arms from the CIA.

And yet this man, Elizardo Sánchez, is optimistic and, perhaps, happy. He recounts some anecdotes. One of his friends in jail told him: "I don't know why I've been arrested; I conspired alone." I laugh, but Elizardo explains that it's more than just a joke. Repression creates an oppressive silence, and amid that oppressiveness, individual attitudes and activities are beginning to emerge that fail to indicate the enthusiasm the regime expects from Cubans. This is regarded as self-conspiracy.

Elizardo claims that the government believes in subjective repression. It's impossible to maintain surveillance over every Cuban, but all Cubans feel as though they're being watched and controlled, and hence persecution mania surfaces more in those who are unorganized and seem like lone conspirators.

Elizardo, however, quickly abandons anecdotes and returns to his dream. And I, for my part, refrain from telling this fine man, Elizardo Sánchez, this lucid, penetrating humanist, that his dream can materialize only after Fidel Castro.

Epilogue

The epilogue begins on February 24, 1965, in Algeria, in what seemed at that moment a theoretical discussion on third-world revolutionary strategy, and wound up being the rope that is hanging Fidel Castro.

Comandante Che Guevara spoke that day as Cuban delegate to the Economic Seminar of the Organization for Solidarity of African and Asian Nations. He developed the thesis that rich Communist countries ought to subsidize nations in the process of organizing their own Communist system. Had he lived twenty years longer, he would have discovered that the Communist nations he regarded as rich weren't in a position to feed their own citizens. Turning *glasnost* to good use, the poet Yevgeny Yevtushenko would, at that later time, denounce the existence of areas in the Soviet Union where, forty years after the Great Patriotic War, bread was still rationed. His words on rationing were censored in *Pravda,* but the *New York Times* published the entire text.

On the occasion of the 1965 Economic Seminar,

Comandante Guevara stated: "The development of countries now embarking on the path to freedom should be subsidized by socialist countries." And: "No longer ought one to talk about developing a mutually profitable trade based on prevailing market prices and unfair international commercial relations imposed on backward countries. If we establish this kind of relationship between both groups of nations, we must accept that socialist countries are, to some extent, accomplices of imperialist exploitation."

The Cuban Revolution was then six years old and, as was already clearly evident, unable to organize an economy that could provide the nation with its basic necessities. Che thought that the solution lay in instilling a new theoretical approach in the Soviet Union toward the idea that Marxist revolutions would break out in the third world over the next couple of decades. Fidel Castro, more pragmatically, realized that Soviet bureaucracy was unenthusiastic about guerrilla romanticism and inclined to favor space satellites over revolutions, and that his own government's inner circle was not immune to the personality cult which presumably had been buried a decade earlier in Khrushchev's speech on Stalin's crimes.

That was Che's last act as a leader in the Castro Revolution. Shortly afterward, he renounced Cuban citizenship, and on April 15, 1965, he disappeared. A few days later, when correspondents questioned Fidel Castro about Che's fate, he replied, "The Comandante is where he is more useful to the Revolution."

Che proved unsuccessful in igniting the wick of any revolution. In April 1967, his rhetoric still enthralled the delegates of the Organization for Solidarity when nations from Asia, Latin America, and Africa met in Havana. His message, dispatched by radio from Bolivia, in whose mountains he had organized a guerrilla group, proclaimed: "How close a shining future could we see if two, three, many Vietnams were to blossom in the world, with their death quotas and vast tragedies, their daily tragedies, their daily acts of heroism and repeated blows against imperialism!" But Bolivia did not become a Vietnam.

Che honestly believed—and he offered his life as proof—that his rhetoric would arouse the scattered, wretched, isolated Bolivian peasants. The Indians of the sierras and valleys listened in bewilderment to this white foreigner, to his strange words and even stranger Spanish, which they failed to understand even after translation. He did not emerge as a revolutionary leader, nor did he become a chief in the Indian villages.

Che died in the guerrilla adventure, but in his own way he signaled the path Fidel Castro was to follow and adapt without acknowledgment: living at the expense of other Communist nations. This didn't necessitate modifying revolutionary theories. On the contrary, those nations had to be assured, in endless speeches, that the U.S.S.R. and its allies continued to be the revolutionary advance guard, and that subsidizing the island was part of a Kremlin-run global strategy.

Castro could not conceive that only two decades later, the Soviet Union would abandon its role as revolutionary advance guard—one that had always been more declamatory than actual—to become an enthusiastic proselytizer for the market economy, corporate profit, the need to take unemployment into account to ensure productivity and efficiency.

In 1974, Castro, having offered Leonid Brezhnev a massive reception contrived to gratify that leader's renowned vanity and frivolity, obtained the sovereign ratification of negotiations begun in 1972, whereby Cuba could postpone its debt payment to the Soviet Union until 1986. Herein may lie the most coherent explanation of the conference organized in 1985 in Havana with the purpose of enabling the third world to declare a general moratorium. Under this umbrella Castro would seek refuge.

He could not imagine that a *perestroika* and a *glasnost*, devised by a man who looked like a successful commercial traveler rather than a bearded revolutionary, would wind up burying Che Guevara's theory. Another aspect of romantic Guevara remained: the refutation of the Soviet Union.

In the course of just two years, Castro switched from generalities to specific accusations. Considering the speed with which transcendental changes are occurring in the Soviet Union, his strategy is recklessly and suicidally naïve. The Soviet Union is facing much graver problems than the presumed loss of a Marxist revolution ninety miles from the United States. And obviously, to overcome these problems, collaboration with the United States is more significant to the U.S.S.R. than Castroist threats.

Cuba Socialista magazine, in its January–February 1987 issue, published another of Castro's speeches, one delivered in the city of Bayamo. Said El Comandante with regard to difficulties in industrial production: "That factory gets wet when it rains. A flat roof was built incorrectly. Conceptually, the solutions weren't the best. There's no reason for making so many flat roofs in a country with heavy rainfall, a tropical country. If flat roofs are made, without the slightest slope, and if these roofs aren't made right, without the proper waterproofing, the roof is transformed into a trench during rainy periods and acts as a hindrance."

But in a speech before the National Assembly in July 1989, the flat roofs achieved international importance. Gorbachev had passed through Havana and informed Castro of the limitations that would be imposed on aid from Moscow. Joseph B. Treaster, the *New York Times* correspondent, reported from Havana that El Comandante had found the guilty party in the matter of the roofs: "Mr. Castro also surprised many Western diplomats by referring in the Assembly to a Soviet-built steel mill 30 miles outside Havana as a 'white elephant,' and saying that flat roofs that had been put on some buildings here on the advice of Soviet technicians were inappropriate in a country with heavy rainfall."

A few days later, in the city of Camagüey, under a persistent rain that forced Castro to cut his speech in celebration of the thirty-sixth anniversary of the attack on the Moncada barracks down to only 110 minutes, he was more explicit. And more apocalyptic: "If one day we awake to the news that the Soviet Union has disintegrated, something we hope never occurs, Cuba and the Revolution will continue to resist." And: "Nor can we state with any certainty that the supplies that have been arriving from the socialist camp with the punctuality of a clock for thirty years will continue to arrive with that same punctuality and regularity."

Oldtime members of the Cuban Communist Party, a party that throughout its history has maintained the closest links to the Kremlin, are extremely leery about entering the dead-end street implicit in Fidel Castro's irresponsible rhetoric. They prefer to refer to a stage of sincere relations as replacing the one-sided relations that prevailed for three decades. But no one ventures to predict the ramifications of this sincerity. If it merely comes down to receiving fewer of the coveted Lada automobiles, El Comandante will harangue the Cubans into using bicycles. But if sincerity means that Moscow will pay for the sugar it buys and charge the going international market prices for oil, the Soviet Union will have accomplished what the United States government has been unable to do in thirty years of diplomacy, crimes, espionage, aggressive acts, and stupidity: the definitive bankruptcy of the Castro regime.

When I was in Cuba in 1987, the press and the leadership were still proceeding with discretion. Vice-President Rodríguez told me that *perestroika* had still not proved that it could yield positive results, which was why Cuba preferred its own Rectification of Errors policy. Nevertheless, he added, *glasnost* was possible in a country unthreatened by foreign dangers: feasible, perhaps, in the Black Sea but never in the Caribbean, less than one hundred miles from the United States.

Every day one reads in the newspaper, hears on radio and television, has it proclaimed in all the schools, that Cuba is prepared to repel a United States invasion, and never is there any mention of the Kennedy-Khrushchev agreement, thus far respected by the two powers, guaranteeing Cuba's territorial integrity.

Two years after that conversation, in which Rodríguez expressed himself with the greatest respect toward the U.S.S.R., Fidel Castro, counteracting the effect created by Rodríguez, banned Cuban distribution of the two most popular Spanish-language Soviet magazines: the weekly *Novedades de Moscú* and the monthly *Sputnik.*

When this announcement was made, *Granma* published one of those lengthy editorials generally attributed to Castro himself, explaining the motives behind the decision: "For over a year the Party administration has found itself obliged on various occasions to reflect on the content of several Soviet publications circulating in this country." The Soviet Union was sending Cuba 15,854,458 copies of thirty-six publications annually.

I underlined the following brief passage from the *Granma* editorial, which analyzes the two magazines:

One discovers in their pages an apology for bourgeois democracy as a supreme form of popular participation, as well as fascination with the North American way of life. Imperialism has disappeared. Those in the Soviet Union today who deny the leading role of the Party and clamor for multipartisanship, who proclaim free market action, encourage foreign investments, rediscover private property, question internationalism and solidarity aid to other countries, are presented in these publications as democratic, radical leftist defenders of the people's interests. Even proponents of the domestic slavery of women are countenanced in these publications. The subversion of values is beyond doubt. Analysis of past and present realities is one-sided. Enemies of Soviet power are nonexistent, only victims. *Novedades de Moscú* and *Sputnik* make way for those who have initiated the attack on Leninism and consistently injure Lenin's image.

I have tried to figure out the Process of Rectification of Errors, as officially inaugurated by Fidel Castro on April 19, 1989, and evolving in the following months through various speeches. I've read most of the speeches, I believe, and studied at length the compilation assembled by Editora Política publishers for its *Olivo* collection.

El Comandante's verbiage is beyond description. The hidden reasons, I suspect, can't be explained by political analysis but must be seen as a kind of mental upheaval, having to do with the psychological relationship between Fidel Castro and other human beings.

In the September 3, 1987, issue of *Granma*, one statement stands out in an item printed in red, a reproduction of a declaration made by Castro ten years earlier at the celebration of the twentieth anniversary of the uprising against Batista in the city of Cienfuegos. The statement: "The Cienfuegos of yesterday was enthusiastic, revolutionary, brave, and heroic; but the Cienfuegos of today—and who's unaware of this?—is a Cienfuegos that's very enthusiastic, very revolutionary, very brave and heroic."

Castro produces several of these statements daily, and believes—and is assured by his friends—that he's creating a new kind of revolutionary conscience. When you go from city to city, from group to group, from person to person, it becomes clear that his rhetoric has produced a vacuum in the conscience of the Cuban people, substituting a stifling collective paranoia. The rest—acceptance, vacillation, informing—is at the service of repression.

Will it be semiotics, rather than history, that definitively judges this strange hegemony of a chief of state?

The Process of Rectification of Errors is not self-criticism; it's an autopsy.

And the epitaph was already discernible in El Comandante's speech at the Fifty-third Plenary National Congress of the Confederation of Cuban Workers, published in early 1987 in *Cuba Socialista:* "We must correct the errors we made in correcting our errors."

The endless labyrinth created by Fidel Castro around the errors committed and the errors about to be committed becomes, in practice, a great, nasty, relentless settling of accounts, an explosive addition to the vortex of intrigue that characterizes every state apparatus. The aim of the Process of Rectification is not reform, even within socialism, a system that isn't working, nor is it replacement of a decrepit leadership, which is precisely what Eastern Europe is attempting to do. The Rectification of Errors is looking for culprits for the disastrous situation its people are living in, and is developing into a huge protective maneuver for El Comandante and his friends.

This perhaps explains why Fidel Castro himself in all his speeches emerges as the initiator of the Rectification of Errors. "I" must be the most utilized word in his pronouncements, along with all the collective and impersonal forms of "I-ism." Some examples: ". . . a total laxity, a chaos that's become truly disturbing, which is why I said it must begin to be rectified" (speech: "The Revolution gets stronger in trials of this kind"). "I've cited an example, not because the head of this firm is bad, or because the workers in this company are bad; they are not to blame; it is we who were turning them into individuals alienated from the Revolution, alienated from conscience, entrusting the building of socialism solely to certain mechanisms. And I myself am going to examine what it is that we were going to build with those methods, what kind of socialism we were going to build via that path" (speech: "In socialism the fundamental factor is the conscience of the nation's men and women"). "I have a great conception of our youth. . . . I shall be very critical, but I also know how to be fair" (speech: "We have the sacred obligation never to be satisfied"). "Here the contradiction between the system of promotion and the quality of teaching became apparent: it became apparent that the criterion of promotion had prevailed, and I in fact had warned against this many times; there must be at least eight or ten speeches where I used the phrase 'Promotion with quality'" (speech: "In the remainder of this century, in the next century and forever, everything depends on the quality of education").

Those who marvel at the number of matriculating university students in Cuba would do well to read a speech by Fidel Castro on education, in which he likewise emphasizes that quantitative indices mean nothing in the presence of low-quality teaching, professor absenteeism, and lack of discipline and laziness on the students' part. The speech was delivered at the Eleventh National Seminar on Education and published in *Granma* on February 17, 1987. As for the caliber of Cuban doctors, medical volunteers from the United States, Latin America, and Western Europe who had to perform alongside them in Nicaragua can attest to their lack of skills.

Advances in the field of education always provided great slogans of the Revolution. As did the development of medical services and hospital aid. And the statistics presented by the Cuban government give the impression of a miracle impossible in any other country. But in a speech at the news conference of the Provincial Committee of the Havana Communist Party, published in *Granma* on January 10, 1987, Castro states with reference to the Frank País Hospital: " . . . the waiting list for important operations is over a thousand, and you cannot but be aware of over a thousand people there, waiting to be operated on, who can't be operated on. . . . It was discovered that the hospitals had no maintenance supplies."

As the Brazilian economist Roberto Campos used to say, statistics are like bikinis: they show what's important but hide what's essential.

I, too, was involved in the neurosis created by Fidel Castro's speeches. A month prior to my arrival, he raised some serious accusations against the popular political leader Luis Orlando Domínguez, in a television message that went on for four-and-a-half hours. An extract of this speech, which I found in the *Granma* files, comprises two thousand words in the July 5, 1987, issue.

I tried to understand the situation.

Castro was making charges against a man who for years had headed the Union of Young Communists, after which he became El Comandante's personal protégé, participating in confidential meetings in the leader's inner cabinet, known as the Team for Coordination and Support. Seldom was any man in Cuba given greater demonstrations of Castro's confidence. Finally he was appointed president of the Civil Aeronautics Institute of Cuba (IACC). But on reviewing Domínguez's life, El Comandante reported in detail that all the tasks his protégé had performed had been done wrong, though he was always forgiven and promoted after the obligatory explanations. Still, to show his constant state of vigilance, Castro didn't overlook mentioning that during those years there was considerable strong criticism of Domínguez's conduct within the team "regarding participation in voluntary work, whether or not he was meeting with colleagues, incidents revealing a certain insensitivity on his part: problems not of the same nature as would subsequently arise."

With equal facility, Castro explained that there had been accusations against Domínguez since November 12, 1985, but that he himself had trusted Domínguez's word and it all sounded like distortion. A year and a half later, bank accounts in Domínguez's name showed up abroad, thousands of dollars in cash in his own home, houses he'd built, even prior to the accusations, for himself and family members, luxury automobiles that he'd acquired for himself and family members, his frivolous, dissipated life.

The Castro brothers like to repeat the fable that they are informed of everything that is going on but occasionally forgive certain deviations in their attempt to save a good but misguided revolutionary. In a dispatch sent from Havana, the Uruguayan journalist Ernesto González Bermejo, editor in chief of the leftist magazine *Brecha*, published in Montevideo, mentions a curious remark concerning General Arnaldo Ochoa. Raúl Castro, reporting to the Tribunal of Honor of the Armed Forces of Cuba, stated: "Beginning in 1970, irregularities began to be noticed in Ochoa's behavior. Apparently he always managed to extricate himself by coming up with an explanation or a joke in the absence of an institutional mechanism that required an objective accounting of his actions, going beyond his friendly or hostile relationship with his superiors." For nineteen years, during which General Ochoa was declared a Hero of the Republic as commander of the Cuban army in Angola and rewarded with the highest honors and privileges, he managed to extricate himself from difficult straits with an explanation or a joke.

My own Cuban-style neurosis began when I tried to learn how a prominent public official could secretly build homes in Havana and at the beach when, in order to obtain a single brick in Cuba, an application must be submitted. How did he manage, secretly, to buy parcels of land, contract architects, have professionals draw up plans, without their commenting on it to some neighbor, friend, or family member; get crews of workers, trucks, cement, furniture, electricity; induce city officials to approve the structures? How could Domínguez and his family, and his wife's family, lead a frivolous, dissolute life in secret? It was impossible to find any halfway acceptable explanation, and so I waited for the trial.

After Fidel Castro's extended accusation and the magnitude of the charges raised by El Comandante against Domínguez, I was surprised that the trial didn't arouse greater interest in the communications media, in conversations, in foreign correspondents' reports. I consulted a lawyer, a state functionary like all lawyers, who assured me that the trial would be oral and public. Foreign correspondents advised me not to go to the courtroom, for the seats would all be filled by the time I arrived. Not attending meant you could transmit only the official version, for any leaks from the courtroom could mean expulsion for the party responsible.

The trial began on Friday, August 28, 1987, and the seats *were* all filled. I thought that some particulars of the defense or further details of the accusation would appear in *Granma,* since Castro had given it such importance. On the appointed day, there was a brief twelve-line announcement that the trial would take place in Section Four of the People's Provincial Court of the City of Havana. The lawyers for the defense would be Drs. Clemente Gómez, Mario Ceballos, and Rafael Garriga. I never got to interview them.

The next day, *Granma* devoted twenty-five lines to the trial, and the only thing new was that Luis Orlando Domínguez and his two accomplices had confessed to all the charges against them.

Two days later, on Monday, August 31, a thirty-eight-line announcement on page one of *Granma* indicated that twenty-two witnesses had confirmed Fidel Castro's accusation. The prosecutor thought that the trial didn't need other witnesses, and the lawyers for the defense concurred with the prosecutor. Domínguez was sentenced to twenty years in jail. I was never able to learn what his statement had been, whether he had named other government members or explained the procedure that implicated scores of functionaries and workers, who incurred risks for the sole purpose of gratifying his wishes. As for the defense lawyers, more than one friend advised me not to be too concerned about finding out what strategy had been followed on the defendant's behalf: the sole mission of the defense is to appeal for clemency, never to look for extenuating circumstances.

I remained, like the Cubans, in the dark, subject to the information provided on television by El Comandante.

Two years after Domínguez's trial, his replacement at the Civil Aeronautics Institute was removed from office and tried. The institute was an important part of the trafficking of drugs from Colombia to the island beaches, and from there in fast boats to Miami.

In many respects, but particularly in the field of drug trafficking, Fidel Castro always enjoyed a credibility far greater than the U.S. government's. When Washington tried to convert the relationship between Cuba and the Colombian cartel into a cause célèbre, it made no headway in circles held to be well informed on the subject of drug trafficking specifically, or Latin America in general.

In any event, the presumed U.S. fantasy or government maneuver was enough to prompt Jeffrey Elliot and Mervyn Dymally, in their interview of Castro in March 1985, to begin with a question pertaining to this accusation:

Mervyn Dymally: The Secretary of State testified before the House Committee on Foreign Relations, and last week an official of the agency for the Control of Narcotics, and also the Consul of the United States Embassy in Mexico, said that they are relying on evidence of an existing drug relationship between Cuba and Colombia.

Commander in Chief Fidel Castro: There's a commandment of God's law that says: "Thou shalt not bear false witness." The present United States administration ought to be constantly reminded of this. Besides, I think that the people and Congress of the United States deserve a little more respect.

It's absolutely impossible for the United States and the Department of State to have a single proof to this effect; I think these are truly foul, infamous methods, a dishonorable form of foreign policy.

Needless to say, the reply wasn't this brief. It fills almost six pages of the book in which the interview was published, and each word points an accusing finger at the United States.

But more revealing of the scant credibility of the United

States government in its accusations against Cuba—often verging, no doubt, on paranoia or on state terrorist tactics—is the report on drugs in the Americas published in 1988 by a prestigious institution, Inter-American Dialogue. This organization of U.S. and Latin American leaders has held meetings since 1982. The report, entitled *The Americas in 1988: A Time of Choices,* was published in conjunction with the Aspen Institute for Humanistic Studies. Out of the five subjects dealt with, one was "Drugs: A Shared Tragedy." Participating in the 1988 dialogue, presided over by Ambassador Sol Linowitz and ex-President Daniel Oduber of Costa Rica, were personalities as varied as Bruce Babbitt, McGeorge Bundy, Robert McNamara, Elliot Richardson, Brent Scowcroft, Cyrus Vance, Carlos Fuentes, Mario Vargas Llosa, and Henry Cisneros. And also an upstart from Argentina, Oscar Camilión, who served the dictatorship loyally: from 1976 to 1981 as ambassador of the military to Brazil, and then as foreign relations minister. As chancellor of the dictatorship, Camilión rigorously contradicted exiled Argentines who denounced the existence of concentration camps where thousands of people disappeared. He is currently United Nations mediator in Cyprus.

"Drugs: A Shared Tragedy" is perhaps one of the most successful chapters in the report. The excellent information it provides is complemented by an evaluation of solutions that can be shared by all. Certain statements justify the concept of a mutual tragedy: "The U.S. Presidential Commission on Organized Crime estimates narcotics sales to total more than $100 billion in the United States, or twice what the United States spends on oil. . . . When narco-dollars buy police, courts, and elected officials, the foundations of democratic rule are shaken. In the struggling democracies of Latin America, when police are offered many times their annual salary to ignore drug dealings, or when honest judges risk death for presiding over drug cases, the threat to representative government is particularly serious. . . . No nation by itself can solve the narcotics problem, and all nations must avoid inflated rhetoric and finger pointing."

Three years after the accusations formulated by the United States, the Inter-American Dialogue report on drugs doesn't mention Cuba, even in a potential relationship, remote or circumstantial, with drug trafficking. In the significant amount of data contained in the report, not even passing mention is made of an existing accusation against Cuba. All the other countries of the continent are analyzed with an abundance of detail regardless of the tenor of their connection with the tragedy: cultivation, distribution, consumption. The countries in the Americas that figure among those accused are: Peru, Bolivia, Colombia, Ecuador, Venezuela, Paraguay, the United States, Mexico, Panama, Brazil, the Dominican Republic, the Bahamas, and Argentina, plus the Cubans of Miami.

In June 1989, barely a year after the report, and four years after Washington's accusations, the General Ochoa scandal bursts forth: the most prominent members of the armed forces and of Cuba's Ministry of the Interior are members of the Medellín cartel. In July, Ochoa and three others are executed after being found guilty of drug smuggling by a military court-martial.

No one, of course, believes it is possible for Cuba, via the armed forces and its security organs, to be a distributor of Colombian drugs without the Castro brothers' participation in the operation. Gradually, or maybe rapidly, given the present crisis of the Cuban regime, the details will come forth, but undoubtedly the global conception of the association with the Medellín cartel doesn't differ from that of the underlying motivation of Peru's Shining Path guerrillas: the acquisition of dollars through the corruption of bourgeois society.

This introduces a new, decisive element into the debate regarding the road that Cuba may take in a peaceful transition toward more humane ways of coexistence, both at home and abroad.

For the reforms to begin from the top seems an increasingly remote possibility. It's hard to imagine the Castros and the current leaders feeling secure enough of survival to take small steps like an amnesty, limited though it might be, for political prisoners who have completed say, half their sentence. Or to allow a glimmer of freedom of the press. Or to introduce reforms in a penal code that accepts a defendant's confession as sufficient proof of his guilt. Or to permit the private practice of law so that the accused may have recourse to defense counsel other than state officials. Or to return to food production in the private sector, provided that it is not to the detriment of collective production.

This is Elizardo Sánchez's dream: peaceful reform, reform that doesn't annul socialism, achieved from above, led by Fidel Castro. Peacefully—that is what is essential.

But the fact is that Elizardo Sánchez is in jail once more. He expressed doubts about the accusations formulated against General Ochoa and his presumed accomplices, he expressed doubts about the confessions of the accused; he believes, as do the family members of those who were shot, that the executions were nothing short of murder. And Elizardo said this aloud.

Poor Elizardo Sánchez! He will never learn to keep his mouth shut. El Comandante had ordained silence. And what happens next remains a frightening unknown.

Jacobo Timerman was born in the Ukrainian town of Bar in 1923, and moved with his family to Argentina in 1928. A life-long journalist, he founded two weekly newsmagazines in the 1960s and was a prominent news commentator on radio and television. He was the editor and publisher of the newspaper *La Opinión* from 1971 until his arrest by military authorities on April 15, 1977. Released in September 1979, he subsequently lived in Tel Aviv, Madrid, and New York. He is the author of *Prisoner Without a Name, Cell Without a Number* and *The Longest War*, which are also available from Vintage. Mr. Timerman returned in 1984 to Buenos Aires, where he lives now.

A NOTE ON THE TYPE

This book was set in Caledonia, a type face designed by W(illiam) A(ddison) Dwiggins (1880–1956) for the Mergenthaler Linotype Company in 1939. Dwiggins chose to call his new type face Caledonia, the Roman name for Scotland, because it was inspired by the Scottish types cast about 1833 by Alexander Wilson & Son, Glasgow type founders. However, there is a calligraphic quality about Caledonia that is totally lacking in the Wilson types.

Dwiggins referred to an even earlier type face for this "liveliness of action"—one cut around 1790 by William Martin for the printer William Bulmer. Caledonia has more weight than the Martin letters, and the bottom finishing strokes (serifs) of the letters are cut straight across, without brackets, to make sharp angles with the upright stems, thus giving a modern-face appearance.

Composed by ComCom, Division of the Haddon Craftsmen, Inc., Allentown, Pennsylvania

Printed and bound by Fairfield Graphics, Fairfield, Pennsylvania